MARKETING

BUSINESS MANAGEMENT ENGLISH SERIES

Comfort, J. and N. Brieger
Finance

Brieger, N. and J. Comfort
Production and Operations

Brieger, N. and J. Comfort
Personnel

Brieger, N. and J. Comfort
Language Reference for Business English

Other ESP titles of interest include:

Brieger, N. and J. Comfort
*Early Business Contacts**

Brieger, N. and J. Comfort
Developing Business Contacts

Brieger, N. and J. Comfort
Advanced Business Contacts

Brieger, N. and A. Cornish
*Secretarial Contacts**

Brieger, N. and J. Comfort
*Technical Contacts**

Brieger, N. and J. Comfort
*Social Contacts**

Brieger, N. and S. Sweeney
The Language of Business English

Davies S. *et al.*
*Bilingual Handbooks of Business
Correspondence and Communication*

McGovern, J. and J. McGovern
*Bank on Your English**

Palstra, R.
*Telephone English**

Palstra, R.
Telex English

Pote, M. *et al.*
*A Case for Business English**

* Includes audio cassette(s)

BUSINESS MANAGEMENT ENGLISH

MARKETING

Jeremy Comfort
and
Nick Brieger

ENGLISH LANGUAGE TEACHING

Prentice Hall International

New York   London   Toronto   Sydney   Tokyo   Singapore

First published 1992 by
Prentice Hall International
Campus 400, Maylands Avenue
Hemel Hempstead, Hertfordshire HP2 7EZ
A division of
Simon & Schuster International Group

Typeset by Keyboard Services, Luton
Printed and bound in Great Britain by Redwood Books, Trowbridge

---

Library of Congress Cataloging-in-Publication Data

Comfort, Jeremy.
  Marketing / Jeremy Comfort and Nick Brieger
    p. cm. – (Business management English series) (English language teaching)
    ISBN 0–13–093469–0
    1. Readers – Business.   2. English language – Business English.
  3. English language – Textbooks for foreign students.   4 Marketing –
  Problems, exercises, etc.   I. Title.   II. Series.   III. Series: English
  language teaching.
  PE1127.B86C66   1991
  428.6′4′02465–dc20
                                                                91–18330
                                                                CIP

British Library Cataloguing in Publication Data

Comfort, Jeremy
  Marketing. – (Business management English series)
  I. Title   II. Brieger, Nick   III. Series
  658.8

  ISBN 0–13–093469–0

5 96

Contents

Introduction

The Business Management English (BME) series comprises four professional content books:

> *Marketing*
> *Finance*
> *Production and Operations*
> *Personnel*

and also *Language Reference for Business English*, which acts as a language and communication reference for the other four titles.

Rationale

The rationale behind the BME series has been to bring together training material in:

- key management disciplines,
- language knowledge, and
- communication skills.

The material is thus designed for:

- specialists who need to develop language and communication skills within their professional areas, and
- non-specialists who wish to extend their knowledge of management areas and develop their language and communication skills.

Marketing

Targets and objectives

This book is aimed at practitioners and students of marketing management: people who need to communicate in English within the increasingly international world of business management. More specifically the material is targeted at non-native speakers of English, with at least an intermediate level in the language, who need to:

- increase their effectiveness in reading and listening in this subject area,
- develop speaking and writing skills around this subject area,
- extend their active vocabulary of both specific marketing terms and more general business English, and
- transfer this knowledge of the language to their own work or study situation.

Organisation of materials

The book and its accompanying cassette are divided into Study Material, Key and Glossary.

STUDY MATERIAL

The Study Material comprises eight units, each of which is divided into two sections (A and B). Each section (A and B) is divided into two parts.

Part 1 is based on a reading task; Part 2 on a listening task. Each part contains the following activities:

1. *Warm-up*
   Questions designed as orientation for the following reading/listening task.

2. *Reading/Listening*
   An input text, together with a task.

3. *Comprehension/interpretation*
   Detailed questions about the input text.

4. *Language focus*
   Language practice exercises – a background explanation is given in *Language Reference for Business English.*

5. *Word study*
   Language exercises to develop professional, business and idiomatic vocabulary.

6. *Transfer*
   A speaking or writing communication task encourages the user to transfer the information presented into his/her own field.

KEY
The Key comprises:

- Tapescripts of the listening extracts.
- Answers to the following activities from the Study Material:
    2. *Reading/Listening* task.
    3. *Comprehension/interpretation* questions.
    4. *Language focus* exercises.
    5. *Word study* exercises.
- Information for the communication activities, where needed.

GLOSSARY

A five hundred word dictionary of marketing. The words have been selected on the basis of frequent usage in this subject area. They are not confined to words used in the book. Simple definitions are followed by an example of usage where appropriate.

Using a unit – activities in each part

1. Warm-up

The questions here will help you to orientate yourself towards the tasks which follow. They encourage you to think about and discuss the subject area.

2. Reading/Listening

(i) *Reading*

Each text has been selected to focus on a key area of professional interest. There is always a task to perform either as you read or just after: this makes the process active. In order to develop your reading skills, you should:

- skim through the text to identify major themes, and
- scan through the relevant paragraphs to complete the task.

Then check your answers with the Key. If they are wrong, read the appropriate section again. The reading task is best done for homework/individual study; the answers can then be discussed in class.

(ii) *Listening*

Each text has been developed to focus on a key area of professional interest. Again there is always a task to perform as you listen to the cassette. In order to develop your listening skills, you should:

- listen all the way through first time, then
- listen again, stopping the cassette to write your answers.

Finally, check your answers with the Key.

3. Comprehension/interpretation

The questions have been developed to:

- check your detailed understanding, and
- encourage you to think more deeply about the subject.

You may need to read/listen again to answer the questions. If you are working in a class, discuss your answers. Finally, check the Key. As you will see, sometimes there is no 'correct' answer.

4. Language focus

This activity focuses on developing your language knowledge. You can do these exercises in class or on a self-study basis. Refer to *Language Reference for Business*

English if you need further information. When you have completed an exercise, check the answers in the Key.

5. Word study

This activity concentrates on developing your word power. You can do this activity in class or on a self-study basis. The answers are in the Key. You may wish to check the Reading or Listening passage to see how the words are used.

6. Transfer

This activity develops your language and communication skills. It is best done in pairs or small groups. You will sometimes find additional information in the Key.

Acknowledgements

The authors would like to acknowledge the advice and support of colleagues at York Associates who gave them the time and space to complete and trial this book.

The publisher and authors would like to acknowledge with thanks the copyright permissions granted for the following publications which were the source of most of the Reading texts in this book:

Principles of Marketing, P. Kotler and G. Armstrong (1988), Prentice Hall.
Marketing Management, P. Kotler (1988), Prentice Hall.

STUDY MATERIAL

UNIT 1
The role of marketing

Section A: What is marketing?

Part 1: Some definitions of marketing

1 Warm-up

1.1 How would you define the function of marketing?

1.2 Do you agree with Peter Drucker when he said, 'The aim of marketing is to make selling superfluous'?

2 Reading

In this section you will find a number of statements about the role of marketing. Read them through, then use them as a basis to formulate your own definition of marketing.

1. 'Marketing is too important to be left to the marketing department.' (David Packard)

2. 'In a truly great marketing organisation, you can't tell who's in the marketing department. Everyone in the organisation has to make decisions based on the impact on the consumer.' (Professor Stephen Burnett)

3. 'Most people mistakenly think of marketing only as selling and promotion. . . . This does not mean that selling and promotion are unimportant, but rather that they are part of a larger *marketing mix*, a set of marketing tools that work together to affect the marketplace.' (Philip Kotler)

4. 'The aim of marketing is to make selling superfluous. The aim is to know and understand the customers so well that the product or service fits him and sells itself.' (Peter Drucker)

5. 'Marketing is a social and managerial process by which individuals and groups obtain what they need and want through creating and exchanging products and value with others.' (Philip Kotler)

6. Marketing is the performance of business activities that direct the flow of goods and services from producer to consumer.'

7. 'Marketing is getting the right goods and services to the right place at the right time at the right price with the right communication and promotion.'

8. 'Marketing is the creation and delivery of a standard of living.'

What would be your own definition of marketing?

3 Comprehension/interpretation

3.1 Which statement suggests that everybody in a company is a marketer?
3.2 Which statement completely discounts the importance of selling?
3.3 Which statement emphasises the role of the four Ps (product, price, place, promotion)?
3.4 Which statement sees marketing more in a sociological role?

4 Language focus

4.1 Adjectives versus adverbs (see Unit 48 in *Language Reference for Business English*)

Look at the following sentences taken from the Reading passage:

'Marketing is too *important* to be left to the marketing department.'
'Most people *mistakenly* think of marketing only as selling and promotion.'

Now complete the sentences below with a word chosen from the following list:

| hard | heavily | late | slightly | well |
| successful | normally | lately | generous | rapidly |

1. Our product is so _____ that we are _____ running out of stock.
2. _____, we invest _____ at this time of year.
3. Profits have only _____ increased and therefore we have had to cut back on further investment.
4. _____, he has been arriving _____ at every meeting.
5. The sales department performed _____ last year so we have given all the sales people a _____ bonus.
6. He worked so _____ that he fell ill.

4.2   Adjective modification (see Unit 49 in *Language Reference for Business English*)

Look at the following sentence taken from the Reading passage:

'In a *truly great* marketing organisation . . .'

Now complete the sentences below by combining two adjectives from the following list. Make any necessary changes.

oriented	complex	tremendous	different
good	radical	sufficient	unusual
qualified	commercial	technical	difficult

1. She's very _____. I think she should get the job.
2. The computer program is _____. I can't understand it.
3. Normally the work is easy. This time it has proved _____.
4. He's _____ but not _____, so he'd make a good engineer but not a salesman.
5. The policy is not _____ from last year. Basically we will try to increase market share.

5   Word study

Complete the list below by inserting the missing forms:

Verb	Noun
to decide	a _____
to _____	sales
to promote	_____
to _____	creation
to exchange	an _____
to _____	performance
to act	an _____
to _____	a producer
to consume	_____
to _____	communication
to deliver	a _____

NOTE: Some of the noun forms above are used without an article (**a/an**). This is because sometimes we want to talk about the concept rather than a particular act or event, for example, compare:

- Sales are falling.
- He got a sale with one of the top manufacturers.

6 *Transfer*

Discuss the following statements:

- The days of the traditional salesman are over.
- The eighties enhanced the role of marketing; the nineties are likely to downgrade it.

Part 2: Some conflicting management philosophies

1 *Warm-up*

1.1 Do you feel all companies must be predominantly market-oriented?
1.2 Is there a danger that if a company is too market-oriented it will ignore other ingredients of success such as efficient production?

2 *Listening*

In this section you will hear a discussion about the direction a certain company should take. There are five participants. Each expresses a different view. These views can be summarised as follows:

A. *The production concept*
    The company should focus on improving production and distribution efficiency.
B. *The product concept*
    The company should focus on making product improvements.
C. *The selling concept*
    The company should focus its effort on selling and promotion.
D. *The marketing concept*
    The company should focus on the needs of its customers.
E. *The societal marketing concept*
    The company should consider the needs not only of its customer but also of society as a whole.

As you listen to the discussion, allocate one of the concepts (A–E) to each of the speakers (1–5):

Speakers	Concept
1	
2	
3	
4	
5	

3 Comprehension/interpretation

3.1 How does speaker 1 aim to bring down prices?
3.2 How does speaker 3 intend to develop a strategy for the future?
3.3 What added dimension does speaker 4 include?
3.4 Why does speaker 5 mention the Japanese?

4 Language focus

4.1 Opinion-giving (see Unit 75 in *Language Reference for Business English*)

Look at the following sentences taken from the Listening passage:

'*I feel* we must certainly ensure quality . . .'
'*As I see the problem*, the major focus . . .'

Now substitute the italicised phrases in the sentences below with the closest equivalent selected from the following list:

I feel	In my opinion	It's certain
We could discuss	What we must do is	I tend to think
I'm sure that	From this point of view	

1. *As I see it*, we should double our development investment.
2. *What we have to do is* withdraw from this sector.
3. *I think* we can't continue as we are.
4. *I'm inclined to believe* we should leave this sector.
5. *I'm convinced that* we must stay in this sector.
6. *We might consider* a gradual withdrawal from the market.
7. *There's no doubt* we can't leave it any later.
8. *From this angle*, we have no alternative.

4.2 Agreeing and disagreeing (see Unit 76 in *Language Reference for Business English*)

Look at the following sentences taken from the Listening passage:

'*I think we'd all agree with you as far as you go.*'
'*I'm not sure I agree with either of you.*'

Now match opposing comments in terms of strength/neutrality/weakness, for example: I agree ↔ I disagree.

1. I think we'd all agree	a. That's interesting but
2. I'm 100 per cent with you!	b. I'm inclined to disagree
3. I can see what you mean	c. There's no way we can agree to that
4. You've got a point	d. I disagree entirely!
5. I tend to agree with you	e. It looks as though there's no agreement
6. We can certainly agree to that	f. I'm not sure I understand your point of view

5 Word study

What are the opposites of the following words and expressions? Use a dictionary if necessary.

1. improvement
2. available
3. competitive
4. effective
5. inside-out
6. investment
7. to bring down prices
8. to stay ahead
9. mass-market

6 Transfer

Discuss the probable management philosophies of the following companies:

- A traditional family-run company manufacturing machine tools.
- A young, high-tech company operating in state-of-the-art electronics.
- A large national utility providing a service throughout the country.

Section B: Marketing planning

Part 1: Strategic planning

1 Warm-up

1.1   Is the profit motive the only real motive for a company's existence?
1.2   What are the dangers to a company of over-planning?

2 Reading

In this section you will find an edited extract from *The Principles of Marketing* (Kotler and Armstrong) entitled 'Strategic planning'. Read it through and complete Charts 1.1 and 1.2.

Strategic planning is the process of developing and maintaining a strategic fit between the organisation's goals and capabilities and its changing market opportunities. It relies on developing a clear company mission, supporting objectives, a sound business portfolio, and co-ordinated functional strategies.

The steps in the strategic planning process are shown in Chart 1.1. At the corporate level, the company first defines its overall purpose and mission. This mission is then turned into detailed supporting objectives that guide the whole

Chart 1.1

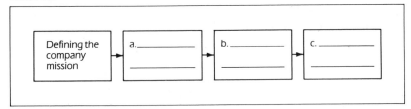

Defining the company mission → a._____ → b._____ → c._____

company. Next, top management decides what portfolio of businesses and products is best for the company, and how much support to give each one. Each business and product unit must in turn develop detailed marketing and other functional plans that support the company-wide plan.

When management senses that the organisation is drifting, it must renew its search for purpose. It is time to ask: What is our business? Who is the customer? What is value to the customer? What will our business be? What should our business be?

Companies traditionally defined their business in product terms such as, 'We manufacture video games', or in technological terms such as, 'We are a chemical-processing firm'. But some years ago, Theodore Levitt proposed that market definitions stated in terms of particular customer groups or needs were better.

Management should avoid making its mission too narrow or too broad. Mission statements should be specific, realistic, and motivating. As an illustration, the International Minerals and Chemical Corporation is in many businesses including the fertilizer business. As you can see in Chart 1.2, the fertilizer division does not say that its mission is to produce fertilizer. Instead, it says that its mission is to 'fight world hunger'. This mission leads to a hierarchy of business objectives, marketing objectives and, finally, marketing strategy.

Chart 1.2

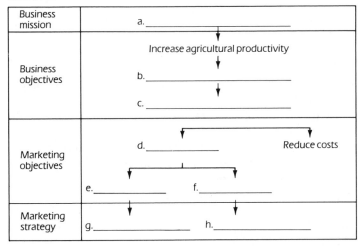

Business mission	a._____
Business objectives	Increase agricultural productivity ↓ b._____ ↓ c._____
Marketing objectives	d._____ ⌐→ Reduce costs e._____ f._____
Marketing strategy	g._____ h._____

The mission of fighting world hunger leads to the company's prime business objective of 'increasing agricultural productivity'. This in turn leads to 'researching new fertilizers which promise higher yields'. But research is expensive and requires improved profits to plough back into research programmes. So a major objective becomes 'to improve profits'.

Profits can be improved by increasing sales or reducing costs. Sales can be increased by enlarging the company's share of the US market and by entering foreign markets. These became the company's current marketing objectives.

Marketing strategies must be developed to support these marketing objectives. To raise its US market share, the company will increase its product's availability and promotion. To enter new foreign markets, the company will cut prices and call on large farms abroad. These are the broad marketing strategies.

3 Comprehension/interpretation

3.1 What is wrong with defining a company's mission in terms of its products or technology?

3.2 Do you think the following mission statement of a pencil manufacturer is too broad or too narrow?

'We are in the communication equipment business'

3.3 Why is improving profits a necessary objective for the fertilizer divison?

4 Language focus

4.1 Sequence (see Unit 67 in *Language Reference for Business English*)

Look at the following sentences taken from the Reading passage:

'The company *first* defines its overall purpose and mission.'
'This mission is *then* turned into detailed . . .'

The following steps describe project management procedure. Put them into the right order.

a. Following these meetings, progress reports must be submitted to the Board.
b. Before final submission of the project report, the project leader should match the findings with original specification.
c. Having agreed investment, the first step is to see what action steps are needed to implement it.
d. As the project nears completion, it is important to outline future steps.
e. Once an action plan has been agreed, select a competent project leader.
f. Finally, the results should be presented to the Board.
g. Once the project has started, regular meetings should be held to monitor progress.
h. The project leader should then call together his or her team and establish clear roles and responsibilities.

4.2   Expressing purpose (see Unit 42 in *Language Reference for Business English*)

Look at the following sentences taken from the Reading passage:

'Sales can be increased *by enlarging* the company's share of the US market . . .'
'*To raise* its market share, the company will increase its product's availability and promotion.'

Now match the purpose with the means:

Purpose	Means
1. In order to reduce labour costs	a. a regular product update was circulated
2. To establish a technological lead	b. research efforts were increased
3. The salesforce was strengthened	c. the workforce was reduced
4. Financial reporting was streamlined	d. by headhunting new salespeople
5. So that customers were kept informed	e. by introducing new accounts software

5   Word study

Find the closest synonym for the words on the left. Select from a–k on the right.

1. purpose	a. drift
2. goal	b. narrow
3. plan	c. reduce
4. reinvest	d. mission
5. wander aimlessly	e. overall
6. sensible	f. objective
7. general	g. increase
8. limited	h. broad
9. wide	i. plough back
10. raise	j. sound
11. cut	k. strategy

6   Transfer

Your task is to present a mission statement for a research-based pharmaceutical company operating world-wide. Select one of the four suggestions below or, if you prefer, develop your own. Present arguments to support your choice.

- To produce quality drugs at the right price.
- To improve the quality of life of mankind.
- To develop new drugs to fight the world's diseases.
- To look after the interests of employees, shareholders and customers.

Part 2: Portfolio analysis

1 *Warm-up*

1.1 Do you feel that the process of conglomeration ('big is beautiful') will continue into the next century?

1.2 What do you see as the dangers of diversification?

2 *Listening*

Listen to the extract from the consultant's presentation. As you listen complete Chart 1.3.

Chart 1.3

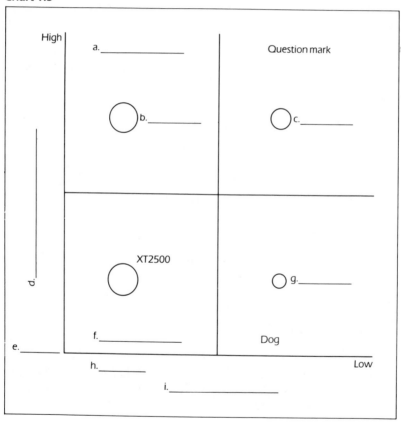

3 Comprehension/interpretation

3.1 Complete the structure of the consultant's presentation:

(i) Analysis of main business areas.

(ii) _____

(iii) _____

3.2 Why are products in the bottom left-hand quadrant called cash cows?

3.3 Why are products in the top right-hand quadrant called question marks?

3.4 Why are products in the top left-hand quadrant called stars?

3.5 What objectives does the consultant propose for the following products:

(i) XT2500

(ii) XT380

(iii) XT25B

(iv) XT25

4 Language focus

4.1 Introductions to presentations (see Skill 1 in *Language Reference for Business English*)

Look at the following sentences taken from the Listening passage:

'*I'm going to divide my presentation into three parts.*'
'*Firstly* an analysis . . .'

Now rearrange the following introduction into a sensible order:

a. If you have any questions, please feel free to interrupt me.

b. Good morning, ladies and gentlemen.

c. I'd like to talk to you today about milk marketing.

d. Finally I'll turn to the question of price.

e. I'll be looking at it from three points of view.

f. How many of you had milk with your breakfast this morning?

g. Firstly, the product and its forms.

h. Perhaps with your cornflakes, maybe with your tea or coffee or even by itself?

i. Secondly, its distribution – in particular door to door deliveries.

4.2 Link phrases for presentations (see Skill 1 in *Language Reference for Business English*)

Look at the following sentences taken from the Listening passage:

'*Right, to start with* the analysis.'
'*So, let's move on to* the next quadrant.'

Now match the phrase with its function:

Phrase
1. By the way
2. As I was saying earlier
3. In a nutshell
4. That deals with the question of distribution
5. I'll come to that point later
6. Let me conclude by saying
7. Let's turn now to the question of
8. There's a further point I'd like to make
9. This brings me to the next point
10. Let me get back to what I was saying

Function
a. To open a new point
b. To close a point
c. To digress
d. To connect two points
e. To refer backwards
f. To refer forwards
g. To return to your structure
h. To make an additional point
i. To summarise
j. To conclude

5 Word study

Decide how many of the words on the right can be combined with the verbs on the left. For example:

to achieve   +   a.   objectives
          +   d.   profits

1. to achieve
2. to generate
3. to launch
4. to phase out
5. to hold
6. to build up
7. to formulate
8. to meet

a. objectives
b. strategy
c. needs
d. profits
e. a product
f. market share

6 Transfer

Write a summary of the consultant's analysis and recommended objectives. Add some possible strategies to achieve these objectives.

UNIT 2
Analysis of market opportunities

Section A: Market research

Part 1: An overview of the market research process

1 Warm-up

1.1   Do you agree with the following statement: 'To manage a business well is to manage the future; and to manage the future is to manage information'?

1.2   Many managers receive too much information. How can organisations ensure that the right information gets to the right people at the right time?

2 Reading

Read the following overview of the market research process. As you read it, complete Charts 2.1 and 2.2.

This section briefly describes the four steps in the market research process, as shown in Chart 2.1: firstly defining the problem and the research objectives, secondly developing the research plan, then implementing the plan, and finally interpreting and presenting the findings.

Defining the problem and research objectives is often the hardest step in the research process. The manager may know that something is wrong, but not the specific causes. For example, managers of a discount retail chain store hastily decided that falling sales were caused by poor advertising. When the research showed that the current

Chart 2.1

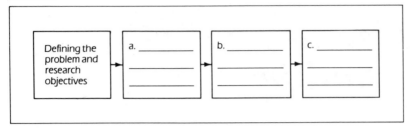

| Defining the problem and research objectives | a. _____ _____ _____ | b. _____ _____ _____ | c. _____ _____ _____ |

advertising was reaching the right people with the right message, the managers were puzzled. It turned out that the stores themselves were not providing what the advertising promised.

When the problem has been carefully defined, the research objectives must be set. The research may be *exploratory* – in order to gather information to better define the problem. It may be *descriptive* – in order to describe market potential, customer attitudes, etc. Sometimes, it may be *causal* – to test hypotheses about cause-and-effect relationships: for example, would a 10 per cent decrease in price lead to significantly higher sales or not?

The second step involves *developing a plan for collecting the information*. The information may be available in the form of secondary data – i.e. it already exists somewhere or it needs to be collected specifically for this project – primary data.

Primary data collection calls for decisions about the research approaches, contact methods, sampling plan and research instruments (see Chart 2.2).

Chart 2.2

Research objectives	Research approaches	Contact methods	Sampling plan	Research instruments
a. _____	d. _____	g. _____	j. _____	m. _____
b. _____	e. _____	h. _____	k. _____	n. _____
c. _____	f. _____	i. _____	l. _____	

There are three main research approaches: the *observational* approach involves gathering information by observing relevant people, actions and situations. For example, a museum checks the popularity of certain exhibits by noting the floor wear around them. This approach is most suited where the objective is exploratory.

For descriptive research, *surveys* are best suited. These can be structured using formal lists of questions asked of all respondents in the same way or unstructured where the interview is guided by the respondent's answers.

Finally for causal research, an *experimental* approach is most effective. Experiments involve selecting matched groups of subjects, giving them different treatments, controlling unrelated factors and checking for differences in group responses.

We will look at contact methods in more detail in Part 2. Briefly, information can be gathered either by mail, telephone or personal interview.

Another decision which has to be made concerns the sampling plan. A sample is a segment of the population selected to represent the population as a whole. There are three variables here: firstly the sample unit, i.e. who is to be sampled? Secondly the sample size, i.e. how many should be surveyed? Thirdly the sampling procedure, i.e. how should the people be chosen: at random, at convenience, on the basis of pre-judgement?

Finally, in developing the research plan, a choice must be made in terms of the research instruments. The most common is the questionnaire. In preparing the questionnaire, the market researcher must decide what questions to ask, the form of the questions (e.g. open/closed, multiple choice), the wording of the questions and their ordering. Although questionnaires are the most common instrument, mechanical instruments such as a galvanometer can be used: this instrument measures the strength of a subject's interest or emotions aroused by and exposure to an advert or a picture.

Once all these decisions have been made concerning the research plan, the researcher must then put it into action. The *implementation* phase is generally the most expensive and the most subject to error. The fieldwork must be monitored closely to make sure the plan is correctly implemented.

The last phase is the *interpretation and reporting*. The researcher should try not to overwhelm managers with statistics, but to present the major findings that are useful in the decisions faced by the management.

3 Comprehension/interpretation

3.1 In the case of the retail chain store, what should the management have done first?

3.2 Can you think of another example of a causal research objective?

3.3 Where could the researcher find secondary data such as competitor information?

3.4 What do you think are the advantages/disadvantages of structured versus unstructured surveys?

3.5 What sort of experimental research could you carry out if you wanted to find out about the relationship between the weather and the incidence of psychological depression?

4 Language focus

4.1 Questions (see Unit 38 in *Language Reference for Business English*)

Look at the following sentences taken from the Reading passage:

'*Who* is to be sampled?'
'*How many* should be surveyed?'
'*How* should these people be chosen?'

Now make questions for the following answers as part of a market research survey:

1. A: My name's Dorothy.
2. A: It's Squires, Mrs Squires.
3. A: Yes, I live here.
4. A: There are four of us. My husband, two daughters and myself.
5. A: No, I don't. I used to work as a nurse before the children were born.
6. A: He's a computer analyst.
7. A: He works for Halfords – a food processing group.
8. A: Yes, we've got two. An Audi and a Peugeot.
9. A: I drive the Audi.
10. A: They're both at school. One's 12, the other 16.
11. A: We usually go to the South of France.
12. A: Two weeks in the summer holidays.
13. A: No, we drive.
14. A: No, not this year. We're going to visit our relatives in the States.

4.2   Modals (see Units 78–81 in *Language Reference for Business English*)

Look at the following sentences taken from the Reading passage:

'The manager *may* know that something is wrong . . .'
'Another decision which *has* to be made . . .'

Now complete the following sentences with an appropriate modal verb:

1. Entrance is forbidden. You _____ not enter.
2. Success is possible. We _____ be successful.
3. Participation is compulsory. We _____ to take part.
4. Permission is given. You _____ take the afternoon off.
5. Success is probable. We _____ succeed.
6. He has the ability. He _____ win the competition.
7. Participation is voluntary. We _____ to go to the reception.
8. Failure is impossible. We _____ fail.
9. It's possible to segment the market. It _____ be segmented.
10. Permission is not given. You _____ leave the building.

5   Word study

A useful way of expanding your active vocabulary is to generate different forms of a word from the base form, for example:

to compete (verb) – competition (noun/concept)
                    – competitor (noun/agent)
                    – competitive (adjective)

Fill in the following table. Use a dictionary if necessary.

Verb	Noun (concept)	Noun (agent)	Adjective
to explore	_____	_____	_____
to respond	_____	_____	_____
to describe	_____	_____	_____
to analyse	_____	_____	_____
to manage	_____	_____	_____
to hypothesise	_____	_____	_____
to observe	_____	_____	_____
to interpret	_____	_____	_____

6 Transfer

Your task is to develop a questionnaire for the following research project.

Definition of problem and objectives

A holiday company wants to assess the potential sales of a new adventure holiday in Scotland. The research objectives are descriptive – to describe/quantify the potential in the male adult population for a one-week adventure holiday involving climbing, canoeing, walking, sailing, etc.

Research plan

To carry out a survey by mail targeted at a sample of adult males between 25 and 40 years old, using a questionnaire, testing the market for a product (specify) or service (specify). Study the sample questionnaire below.* Develop a short questionnaire (maximum 10 questions) along similar lines.

Part 2: Contact methods used in market research

1 Warm-up

1.1   Would you fill in a market research questionnaire sent to you by mail?
1.2   Do you always respond honestly to market research interviews?

2 Listening

Listen to the discussion about contact methods in market research. As you listen, complete the Chart 2.3 using the following code to signify the strengths and weaknesses of the three methods:

✓✓ = excellent   O = satisfactory
✓ = good   X = poor

* For Language Training services, consider the nature of the questions, their sequence and the reasons for them.

QUESTIONNAIRE

Name _____ Position held in Company _____

Company _____ Nature of Business _____

Which statement reflects your current position with business abroad?

We import and export goods/services ☐
We import goods/services only ☐
We export goods/services only ☐
We are looking to export or import ☐
Other (please state) ☐ _____

Which of the following countries do you trade/hope to trade with?

G☐   F☐   D☐   I☐   J☐   Sp☐   Sw☐   No☐   Da☐
Other (please state) _____

Of the services we provide, which ones would you like to know more about?

Translation   Interpretation   Language Training
Business Seminars   Hotline   Open Learning Centre

Have you or other members of staff used any of the following language services in the past year?

Self-learning books/audio cassettes ☐
Another local language centre ☐
Lectures at educational institutions ☐
National schemes (e.g. Berlitz) ☐

Were you or your staff satisfied with the training in terms of the help it gave to your business?

Very satisfied ☐   Quite satisfied ☐   Satisfied ☐   Dissatisfied ☐

Before you received this brochure pack, had you heard of York Associates?

Yes ☐   No ☐

If yes, then how? _____

Chart 2.3

	Mail	Telephone	Personal
1. Flexibility 2. Amount of data that can be collected 3. Control of interviewer bias 4. Control of sample 5. Speed of data collection 6. Response rate 7. Cost			

3 Comprehension/interpretation

3.1 What is meant by interviewer bias?

3.2 Why is the response rate very low for mail questionnaires?

3.3 What is the difference between a street interview and a focus group?

4 Language focus

4.1 Comparison of adjectives (see Unit 50 in *Language Reference for Business English*)

Look at the following sentences taken from the Listening passage:

'The cost will be considerably *lower* than the other methods.'
'You tend to get *more honest* answers . . .'

Now complete the following sentences using the adjective in brackets:

1. Our production methods have become much _____. (modern)
2. It's become _____ to forecast our results. (easy)
3. My new job is much _____. (interesting)
4. We did a lot _____ than we expected. (good)
5. He couldn't have done _____. (bad)
6. We need to use a _____ approach than we have been employing. (direct)
7. Our aims have become much _____ as the market has become more segmented. (narrow)
8. I feel the problem is _____ than you are saying. (superficial)
9. It's _____ than we anticipated. (funny)
10. Our share is slightly _____ than forecast. (high)

4.2 Adjective modification – degree (see Unit 49 in *Language Reference for Business English*)

Look at the following sentences taken from the Listening passage:

'Mail questionnaires are *much* less flexible . . .'
'It's *a lot* more flexible . . .'

Now classify the following modifiers as: (A) strong, (B) neutral, (C) weak.

1. moderately
2. a little
3. slightly
4. considerably
5. quite a lot
6. a lot
7. much
8. somewhat
9. a bit

5 Word study

Complete the table below with suitable adjectives:

Concept	Adjective	Opposite adjective
size	large/big	small
cost	_____	_____
honesty	_____	_____
flexibility	_____	_____
speed	_____	_____
quality	_____	_____
quantity	_____	_____
accuracy	_____	_____

NOTE: In many cases there is more than one possible adjective.

6 Transfer

Write a short memo comprising:

- a summary of different contact methods,
- conclusions on the best method, and
- a recommendation for the choice of method and its implementation.

Section B: The market environment

Excellent companies take an outside-in view of their business. They monitor the changing environment and continuously adapt their businesses to their best opportunities. The marketing environment comprises the 'non-controllable' actors and forces that affect a company's markets and marketing.

Part 1: Competitors

1 Warm-up

1.1 Do you think the commercial world has become more competitive during the past twenty years? If so, why?

1.2 Besides companies which sell similar products, what other types of competitor does an organisation face?

2 Reading

Read the following extract about the actors in a company's micro-environment. As you read it, complete Chart 2.4 which illustrates four types of competitor.

The major actors in a company's micro-environment are the company itself, suppliers, market intermediaries, customers and competitors. We will briefly define what we mean by these actors and then look in more detail at competitors.

The company
All of the departments within a company (e.g. finance, production, human resources) have an impact on the marketing department's plans and actions.

The suppliers
Developments in the supplier environment, such as prices and availability of raw materials, have a substantial impact on a company's marketing operations.

The market intermediaries
Middlemen such as agents, wholesalers and retailers, are powerful and important actors. In some cases they can dictate terms and even, if treated badly, bar the manufacturer from certain markets.

Customers
(The behaviour of consumers will be looked at in more detail in the next unit.)

Competitors
A company's marketing system is surrounded by a host of competitors. The best way for a company to grasp the full range of its competition is to take the viewpoint of a buyer. Let us consider the case of a chocolate bar manufacturer. Suppose a person has been working hard and needs a break. The person asks, 'What do I want to do now?'

Among the possibilities that pop into his or her mind are socialising, exercising and eating (see Chart 2.4). We will call these *desire competitors*. Suppose the person's most immediate need is to eat something. Then the question becomes, 'What do I want to eat?' Different foods come to mind, such as potato chips, candy, soft drinks, and fruit. These can be called the *generic competitors* in that they represent different basic ways to satisfy the same need. At this point the person decides on candy and asks, 'What type of candy do I want?' Different candy forms come to mind such as chocolate bars, licorice, and sugar drops. They all represent *product form competitors*. Finally the consumer decides on a chocolate bar and faces several brands such as Hershey, Nestlé and Mars. These are the *brand competitors*.

Chart 2.4   Four types of competition

Desire competitors	a. _____ _____	f. _____ _____	j. _____ _____
For example: Socialising Exercising Eating	For example: b. _____ c. _____ d. _____ e. _____	For example: g. _____ h. _____ i. _____	For example: k. _____ l. _____ m. _____

Unfortunately company executives tend to focus primarily on the brand competitors and on the task of building brand preference. In fact, companies are myopic if they focus only on their brand competitors. The real challenge is to expand their primary market (in the above case the candy market) rather than simply fight for a larger share in a fixed-size market.

3   Comprehension/interpretation

3.1   What effect could a cost-conscious finance department have on a marketing plan?

3.2   What effect could a supply shortage have on the launch of a new product?

3.3   Why do companies use wholesalers and retailers rather than supplying their customers direct?

4   Language focus

4.1   Present simple (see Unit 2 in *Language Reference for Business English*)

Look at the following sentences taken from the Reading passage:

'The person asks, "What *do I want* to do now?"'
'The consumer *decides* on a chocolate bar . . .'

Generalise from the following specific statements and questions. For example:
What are you doing? → *What do you do?*

1. He's skiing in the Alps. → _____ every winter.
2. What would you like to eat? → _____?
3. I'm living with my parents. → _____.
4. Would you like a coffee? → _____?
5. She's working very hard. → _____.
6. Are you finding this exercise difficult? → _____?
7. The marketing plan is working well. → _____.
8. Are we gaining market share? → _____?
9. Would you prefer the window open? → _____?
10. She is losing the race. → _____.

4.2   Universal conditions (see Unit 10 in *Language Reference for Business English*)

Look at the following sentences taken from the Reading passage:

'Companies *are* myopic if they *focus* only on their brand competitors.'

Now create sentences that express universally true statements by matching statement with condition. The first one has been done for you.

Statement	*Condition*
Companies fail	not motivated
Machines break down	no competition
Good employees leave	not growing
Product quality falls	ignore customers' needs
Productivity rises	properly maintained
A company regresses	incentive scheme exists

1. *Companies fail if they ignore customers' needs.*

5   Word study

Imagine you are developing a marketing plan for the launch of a new sports car.
Use the analysis above to classify the following into the four types of competitor:
desire, generic, product form and brand competitors.

Ferrari	turbo
convertible	estate car
a luxury holiday	Jaguar
family saloon	2 + 2
a swimming pool	sports car
Toyota	Porsche

6 Transfer

You work in a team developing a marketing plan for a new health care product – dental chewing gum. Your task is to identify all the competitors for this product. Use the above analysis to identify your competitors and then prepare a presentation outlining the major opportunities and threats posed by your competition.

Part 2: Publics

1 Warm-up

1.1   How important do you feel a company's image is in terms of product sales?
1.2   Do you think pressure groups such as environmentalists have a positive or negative influence on a manufacturing company's development?

2 Listening

Listen to an extract from a meeting between a marketing director and his public relations manager. They are talking about the company's planned PR activities. As you listen, complete Chart 2.5.

Chart 2.5

Publics	Planned action
Financial institutions Media Government Pressure groups Local community General public Employees	

3 Comprehension/interpretation

3.1   What does PR stand for?
3.2   Why does the company organise a press conference when the six-monthly results are announced?
3.3   What does the legal department do regarding government legislation?
3.4   Why do you think the 'Greens' will be pleased about the closure of the plant?

4 Language focus

4.1 Present continuous – future reference (see Unit 1 in *Language Reference for Business English*)

Look at the following sentence taken from the Listening passage:

'Our press relations officer *is organising* a press conference in a couple of months' time . . .'

Now change the following sentences so that they express *fixed arrangements* rather than *intentions*:

1. The managing director *is going to fly* to Dubai next week.
2. The production department *aims to install* a new machine next month.
3. What *are you planning to do* at the weekend?
4. The chairman *intends to resign* in the next few months.
5. The marketing department *plans to move* offices soon.
6. Which market *do you intend to concentrate on* next year?
7. Our strategy *is going to be implemented* during the year.
8. We *aim to increase* prices during the next quarter.

4.2 **Going to** – future reference (see Unit 9 in *Language Reference for Business English*)

Look at the following sentences taken from the Listening passage:

'There's *going to be* a piece about the drug . . .'
'It'*s going to be* important . . .'

Now read through the following dialogue. Correct the verbs in italics if you think it necessary:

A: How's the press release *going*?
B: Oh, I haven't finished it yet. Don't worry, it'*s going to be* ready on time.
A: Good. I've got a meeting with the ad agency tomorrow at 9. *Could you come?*
B: Just a moment. I'*m going to look at* my diary . . . Yes, that'*s going to be* okay. What *will you discuss?*
A: We *will talk* about the new campaign.
B: Right, I'*m certainly going to be* there.
A: Great. Look, I *will go* to lunch in half an hour. What about talking it over together first?
B: Sorry, I've got another appointment at lunch. We *could meet* later this afternoon, if you like?
A: Okay, let's say 4 o'clock in my office.
B: Fine, I'*m going to be* there.

5 Word study

Find the best synonym. Match the words and expressions on the left with those on the right.

1. legislation		a.	an opinion
2. to brief		b.	to prepare
3. a piece		c.	a matter
4. to sponsor		d.	laws
5. to lobby		e.	six-monthly
6. unease		f.	to inform
7. voice		g.	anxiety
8. spokesperson		h.	to take care of
9. closure		i.	to support
10. issue		j.	a shut-down
11. to look after		k.	to influence
12. twice yearly		l.	part of a programme
13. to draw up		m.	a representative

6 Transfer

Now write a press release based on the activities planned by the PR department.

UNIT 3
Buyer behaviour and market segmentation

Section A: Buyer behaviour

Part 1: Consumer buyer behaviour

1 Warm-up

What differences in buyer behaviour would you expect with the following two products?

- A family annual holiday
- A tennis racket

2 Reading

Read the following extract about consumer buying roles and decision behaviour. As you read, complete Charts 3.1 and 3.2.

The marketer needs to know what people are involved in the buying decision and what role each person plays. For many products, it is fairly easy to identify the decision-maker. Men normally choose their own shoes and women choose their own make-up. However, other products and especially new ones may well involve a decision-making unit of more than one person.

Consider the selection of a family car. The initial suggestion might come from the oldest child – he or she would be the *initiator*; a friend or colleague might advise the family on the kind of car to buy – he or she would be the *influencer*; the husband could be the one to choose the make while the wife might have a definite opinion regarding the car's style – they would be the *deciders*; the husband may well be the one actually to buy – the *buyer*; the wife might end up using the car more than her husband – she'd be the *user*.

Chart 3.1

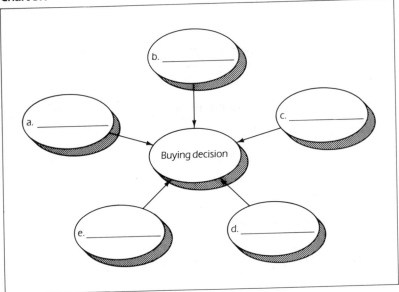

A company needs to identify who occupies these roles because they affect product design and advertising message decisions. The car manufacturer in this case might be wise to include all the above participants in an advertisement.

The more complex buying decisions are likely to involve more buying participants and more buyer deliberation. Chart 3.2 identifies three types of buying behaviour.

Routine response behaviour occurs when consumers buy low-cost, frequently purchased items. They know a lot about the product class and major brands and they have fairly clear brand preference. The goods in this class are often called low-involvement goods. A household detergent would fall into this category. Marketers of products that consumers buy routinely have two tasks. First, they must satisfy current customers by maintaining consistent quality, service and value. Second, they must try to attract new buyers – break them out of the routine of buying competing products – by introducing new features and using point-of-purchase displays and price discounts.

Buying is more complex when buyers confront an unfamiliar brand in a familiar product class. *Limited problem-solving* is involved when the consumer is fully aware of the product class but is not familiar with all the brands and their features. Buying a tennis racket might fall into this bracket. Marketers must design a communication programme that will help buyers understand the company's brand and give them confidence in it.

Sometimes buyers face complex buying decisions for more expensive, less frequently purchased products in a less familiar product class. In these situations, buyers use *extensive problem-solving* to find out about the product class and the brands available. Buying a new stereo system might fall into this category. Marketers of products in this class need to help buyers learn about important buying criteria and persuade them that their brands rate high in terms of important features and benefits.

Chart 3.2

Behaviour type	Product features	Product example	Marketing tasks
1.			
2.			
3.			

3 Comprehension/interpretation

3.1 Which of the buying roles do you consider the most important in the purchase of a new car?

3.2 What other examples of low-involvement goods can you think of?

3.3 What other examples of products in the limited problem-solving class can you think of?

3.4 What other examples of products in the extensive problem-solving class can you think of?

4 Language focus

4.1 Scale of likelihood (see Unit 80 in *Language Reference for Business English*)

Look at the following sentences taken from the Reading passage:

'The initial suggestion *might* come from the oldest child . . .'
'The husband *could* be the one to choose . . .'
'The husband *may well* be the one actually to buy . . .'

Now complete the following sentences according to the 'probability' indicated in brackets:

1. We _____ achieve 25 per cent market share. (probable)
2. We _____ reach our targets this year. (impossible)

3. Prices _____ fall over the next two months. (certain)
4. Interest rates _____ also come down. (possible)
5. Sales _____ to rise above 40 million. (improbable)
6. Unemployment _____ to rise to nearly 2 million. (probable)
7. Salaries _____ not go up this year. (possible)
8. Fixed costs _____ not be reduced any further. (impossible)

4.2   Advice (see Units 78 and 81 in *Language Reference for Business English*)

Look at the following sentences taken from the Reading passage:

'They *must* satisfy current customers . . .'
'Marketers of products in this class *need to* help buyers learn about . . .'

Now give strong advice in the following situations. Complete the sentences:

1. Product quality is falling. You _____ product quality.
2. Profitability is declining. You _____ costs.
3. Your top salespeople are leaving. You _____ better salaries.
4. Your deliveries are always late. You _____ delivery times.
5. Your products are too expensive. You _____ prices.
6. You're growing too fast. You _____ your growth.
7. The product is not sufficiently well known. You _____ advertising.
8. Demand exceeds supply. You _____ production.

5 Word study

Building word groups is one way of extending your active vocabulary. Fill the spaces in the table using words from the following list:

suggest   advise   influence   engaged
long-winded   identify   usual   complex
propose   thorough   motivated   interested
choose   regular   often   select

persuade	decide	extensive	routine	involved
_____	_____	_____	_____	_____
_____	_____	_____	_____	_____
_____	_____	_____	_____	_____
_____				

6 Transfer

Now identify the consumer roles and behaviour which apply in the case of the following product:

- Up-market holiday location: Bali
- Holiday complex on coast
- Children not encouraged

Part 2: Organisational buyer behaviour

In this part we will look at one aspect of the industrial buying process: making decisions about suppliers.

1 Warm-up

1.1 What differences do you think there are between consumer and industrial buying behaviour?

1.2 How important do you think relationships (personal factors) are in the industrial buying process?

2 Listening

Listen to the discussion among three members of a purchasing department. As you listen, indicate the ranking (1–3) they give to the factors identified in Chart 3.3; 'A', the first speaker is Mark, 'B' is the chairman, 'C', the second speaker is Peter.

Chart 3.3

	Routine purchases			Special purchases		
	A	**B**	**C**	**A**	**B**	**C**
Delivery capability						
Quality						
Price						
Repair service						
Technical capability						
Financial strength						

3 Comprehension/interpretation

3.1 Why does the first speaker prioritise financial strength?

3.2 Why do you think he feels price is not such an important factor in the case of special purchases?

3.3 Why is the chairman surprised that neither of the previous speakers have prioritised repair service?

3.4 Why does the chairman need to agree on a ranking for these factors?

4 Language focus

4.1 Conditionals (see Unit 10 in *Language Reference for Business English*)

Look at the following sentence taken from the Listening passage:

'If I *had to choose* for our routine purchases, I*'d put* quality first . . .'

Make theoretical or hypothetical statements about the following situations:

Condition		Outcome/action
demand slumps	→	increase advertising
poor weather	→	sales decrease
war breaks out	→	scale down production
boss resigns	→	get his job!
strike	→	negotiate with unions
stop smoking	→	much healthier

1. *If demand slumped,* _____

4.2 Either/neither (see Unit 60 in *Language Reference for Business English*)

Look at the following sentences taken from the Listening passage:

'I'm not sure I agree entirely with *either of you.*'
'I'm surprised *neither of you* mentioned repairs.'

Complete the following sentences with:

either   neither   too   nor   or   both

1. John and Sarah _____ agree. Peter does _____.
2. _____ Simon _____ Ann agree with you. They _____ think you are crazy.
3. You can _____ leave the firm of your own free will _____ be fired. In any case, I want you out.
4. _____ Peter _____ Roger like living in London. I don't like it _____.
5. _____ Marketing and Production share the same opinion about the need for higher quality. However, _____ of them have come forward with any concrete proposals.

5 Word study

The six criteria are listed below. Match the adjectives with criteria to which they may apply:

Criteria
1. Delivery capability

2. Quality

3. Price

4. Repair service

5. Technical capability

6. Financial position

Adjectives
a. experienced
b. sound
c. punctual
d. assured
e. expensive
f. efficient
g. weak
h. skilled
i. delayed
j. reasonable
k. poor
l. reliable
m. unstable
n. cheap
o. slow
p. excellent
q. friendly
r. up-to-date

6 Transfer

Below is an extended list of supplier attributes. Draw up your own system of weighting (prioritising) for the ten most important attributes. Write a short memo explaining why you have decided on this order.

Delivery capability
Quality
Price
Repair service
Technical capability
Financial strength
Production facilities
Reputation

Training aids
Management and organisation
Packaging capability
Moral/legal issues
Geographical location
Labour relations record
Communications
Attitude towards buyer

Section B: Market segmentation: targeting and positioning

Markets can be segmented on the basis of geography, demography, social class, consumer behaviour, etc.

Part 1: Targeting of segments

1 Warm-up

1.1 What type of product might be targeted at the whole market (without considering different segments)?

1.2 What are the advantages of mass-marketing?

2 Reading

Read the following extract about market targeting. As you read, complete Chart 3.4.

Undifferentiated marketing

The company might decide to ignore market segment differences and go for the whole market with one market offer. This approach focuses on what is common in the needs of consumers rather than on what is different. Product and marketing programmes are designed to appeal to most buyers. Mass distribution and mass advertising are relied on. An example of undifferentiated marketing would be the launch of a new chocolate bar targeted at everyone.

This approach provides cost economies. Production, inventory and transportation costs are kept low by the single product line. Similarly, advertising, market research and product management costs are kept low. However, most modern marketers have strong doubts about this strategy. It is very difficult to develop a product or brand that will satisfy all consumers. Heavy competition will usually be attracted and therefore margins will often be low.

Differentiated marketing

A company may decide to target several market segments and design separate offers for each. General Motors tries to produce a car for every 'purse, purpose and personality'. By establishing a strong position in several segments, consumers' overall identification with the company will be strengthened and therefore provide a better chance of repeat purchasing. Differentiated marketing typically creates more total sales than undifferentiated marketing. But the production and marketing costs are increased. In some cases, 'oversegmentation' can occur and a company may try to broaden its base. For example, the target market for Johnson & Johnson's baby shampoo was broadened to include adults.

Concentrated marketing

Many countries see a third possibility that is especially appealing when company resources are limited. Instead of going for a small share of a large market, the firm goes for a large share of a submarket. Many examples of concentrated marketing can be found. In computers, Sinclair targeted the bottom end of the home computer market; in cars, Saab focuses on the luxury sports car market; in clothes, Laura Ashley originally targeted a distinct segment of the women's clothes market.

Through this approach, a strong market position can be achieved, operating costs can be kept low and, if targeted well, the firm can earn a high rate of return on its investment. At the same time, higher than normal risks are involved. The particular market segment can turn sour; larger competitors may well enter the same segment with many more marketing resources. For these reasons, many companies prefer to diversify in several segments.

In terms of application, many factors must be considered when choosing one of the above strategies. When a firm's resources are limited, concentrated marketing makes the most sense. Undifferentiated marketing is more suited when the product is homogeneous like grapefruit or steel. The product's stage in its life cycle must also be considered. When a new product is introduced, it is often practical to launch just one version and in that case undifferentiated or concentrated marketing makes the most sense. Differentiated marketing is more applicable to maturer products. Finally, competitors' marketing strategies are important. It can be suicidal to use undifferentiated marketing when the competitors are actively segmenting the market. Conversely, when the competitors are using undifferentiated marketing, a firm can gain by using differentiated or concentrated marketing.

Chart 3.4

Targeting strategy	Definition	Example	Advantages	Disadvantages
Undifferentiated				
Differentiated				
Concentrated				

3 Comprehension/interpretation

3.1 What other products besides a chocolate bar would benefit from undifferentiated marketing?

3.2 Do you feel that most customers develop brand loyalty where a company offers a complete range of products?

3.3 Why do many companies prefer to diversify rather than stay in a concentrated market?

3.4 Why is differentiated marketing more suitable for products which are in the mature stage of their product life cycle?

4 Language focus

4.1 Active versus passive (see Units 21 and 22 in *Language Reference for Business English*)

Look at the following sentence taken from the Reading passage:

'Through this approach, a strong market position *can be achieved*, . . . and the firm *can earn* a high rate of return . . .'

Now change the following sentences from active voice to passive or vice versa:

1. We might ignore market segment differences.
2. A marketing programme can be designed to appeal to most buyers.
3. You can keep transportation costs low by a single product line.
4. Several market segments may be targeted.
5. More total sales are created by differentiated marketing.
6. A company may broaden its base.
7. Many examples of concentrated marketing can be found.
8. Sinclair targeted the bottom end of the market.
9. The segment may be attacked by larger competitors.
10. Many factors must be considered when choosing a strategy.
11. We would have considered the identification of a niche.
12. Down-market products could have been added to the product range.

5 Word study

Match up the verbs on the left with an appropriate word or phrase on the right:

1. to ignore	a. your base
2. to go	b. on the luxury end of the market
3. to appeal	c. advice
4. to attract	d. to maturer products
5. to establish	e. sour
6. to broaden	f. in several markets
7. to earn	g. for a particular market
8. to turn	h. to all consumers
9. to diversify	i. the bottom end of the market
10. to target	j. a high rate of return
11. to apply	k. competition
12. to focus	l. a strong position

6 Transfer

Your company wants to develop and market a new dental chewing gum. It will be designed to attack plaque and be eaten after meals. It will be pleasant to chew.

Decide which market segments to target and which approach to use. Present arguments to support your decision.

Part 2: Positioning in a segment

1 Warm-up

Some companies produce very similar products (e.g. a number of brands of detergent) under different names and then position them differently in the same market. What are the advantages of doing this?

2 Listening

Listen to the product management meeting. They are discussing how the new dental gum should be positioned in the market. As you listen, use Chart 3.5 to indicate the preferences of the speakers.

Chart 3.5

Positioning	Speaker 1	Speaker 2	Speaker 3

Product attributes:
  a. prevents decay
  b. minty taste
 	
Usage: after meals
 	
Competitive advantage:
  Company image			

3 Comprehension/interpretation

3.1 How long have they been developing Dentigum?

3.2 When was Dentimint launched?

3.3 What monthly sales figure has Dentimint been achieving?

3.4 What supports speaker 1's argument in favour of usage positioning?

3.5 How long has their company been in dental care?

3.6 What is the danger of stressing the breakthrough in a new product class area?

4 Language focus

4.1 Present perfect versus past simple (see Units 3 and 5 in *Language Reference for Business English*)

Look at the following sentences taken from the Listening passage:

'Dentigum *has been developed* over the last two years.'
'Dentimint *was launched* four months ago.'

Now complete the following sentences by putting the verbs into either the present perfect or the past simple:

1. We _____ (reach) our targets last year.
2. Sales _____ (fall) since the beginning of June.
3. Contracts _____ (be signed) but work _____ (not begin) yet.
4. The marketing department _____ (recruit) two new assistants so far this year.
5. We _____ (start) the advertising campaign last month and since then sales _____ (rocket).
6. Our research _____ (be carried out) last year but I still _____ (not see) the results.
7. Turnover _____ (rise) dramatically since we _____ (be founded).
8. We _____ (expect) a fall in profits last year as our costs nearly _____ (double).
9. We _____ already (sell) more units this year than we _____ (do) in the whole of last year.
10. He _____ (feel) we should _____ (not take on) so many salespeople last year.

4.2 Present perfect continuous (see Unit 6 in *Language Reference for Business English*)

Look at the following sentence taken from the Listening passage:

'Dentimint *has been achieving* monthly sales of 50,000.'

Now decide which of the following verbs can be put in the present perfect continuous in order to stress the ongoing nature of the event. Make the necessary changes:

1. Liverpool has won all its matches this season.
2. Liverpool has played very well this season.
3. We have sold 250 units this quarter.
4. Our sales strategy has worked very well.
5. It has rained all day.
6. It has been cold since March.
7. He has been ill for two days.
8. I've tried to telephone you all day.
9. We have survived the competition.
10. Prices have fallen from 15p a unit to 12p.

5 Word study

Use the appropriate forms of the words/expressions below to complete the text:

> to beat someone to it
> a breakthrough
> to be in the field of
> household name
> track record
> to make something of
> to build a customer base
> to trade on

Grade Health Care have an impressive 1. _____. They were the first 2. _____ of anti-rheumatic drugs when they made a 3. _____ in the treatment of arthritis. Some of their drugs in this field have become so well-known that they are 4. _____. They are now able to 5. _____ their name in this field to launch drugs in other areas. Although one of their competitors – Smithsons – 6. _____ it when they launched a new antibiotic, Grade have 7. _____ in this area too. They were able to 8. _____ of their antibiotic by stressing their reputation in other health areas.

6 Transfer

Write a short report summarising the targeting and positioning you recommend for Dentigum.

UNIT 4
Products

Product planners need to think about their products on three levels. The most basic level is the core product – what is the buyer really buying? Marketers must uncover the needs hiding under every product and sell benefits not features. The core product has to be turned into a tangible product. This may have as many as five characteristics: features, a brand name, styling, packaging and quality levels. Finally, the product may offer additional services and benefits that make up an augmented product. These aspects of a product are illustrated in Chart 4.1.

Chart 4.1

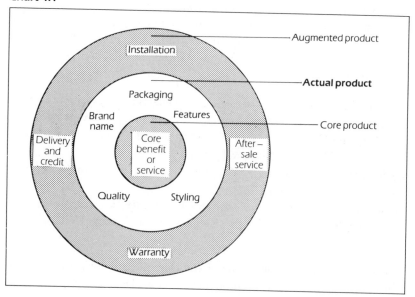

Section A: Product type and mix decisions

Part 1: Branding decisions

1 Warm-up

1.1 When you're at the supermarket, do you generally buy branded products? If so, why?

1.2 How do you identify products? By their name, their packaging?

2 Reading

Read this extract about brand decisions. As you read it, complete the brand decision flowchart in Chart 4.2.

Brand decisions are an important part of product strategy. The company must first decide: Do we develop a brand or not? Historically, most products went unbranded. However, today branding has grown so strong that almost everything is branded. Apart from a phase in the late '70s when there was a return to unbranded or generic products, a brand name has become a vital part of a product's identity.

The issue of branding raises some questions. Why have branding in the first place? Who benefits from branding? How do they benefit? What is the cost of branding?

Having decided to brand a product, the manufacturer has three sponsorship options: Do we launch it under the manufacturer's own label? Would it be better to launch it through middlemen under a private label? Or should we combine these two strategies and use both labels? As an example, in the fashion industry the use of private labels has increased dramatically and some marketers predict that middlemen's brands will eventually knock out all but the strongest manufacturer's brands.

Manufacturer's who brand their products face several further choices. There are at least four brand-name strategies:

1. They could go for an *individual brand name*. This policy is normally adopted in the toiletry market where buyers are often unaware of the manufacturer's name.
2. They could go for a *blanket family name* for all products. This policy is followed by companies such as Heinz and Black & Decker.
3. They could go for *separate family names* for product classes. For example, Beecham uses Silvikrin for all hair shampoos.
4. They could go for the *company trade name combined with the individual product name*. This policy is followed by Kellogg's (Kellogg's Corn Flakes, Kellogg's Rice Crispies)

Two of the questions which must be answered are: Does the company want to tie its name and therefore reputation to the product's success? Do we want to save on advertising costs in the long run by establishing a strong family name for a line of products?

Finally, we come to the actual choice of name. Most large marketing companies have developed a formal brand name selection process. In all cases these are some of the questions which must be asked about a proposed name?

1. Does it suggest something about the product's benefits and qualitites?
2. Is it easy to pronounce, recognise and remember?
3. Is it distinctive – does it stand out from its competitors?
4. Does it translate easily into other languages?
5. Can it be registered for legal protection? Brand names which infringe on existing brands or are merely descriptive may be unprotectable.

Chart 4.2

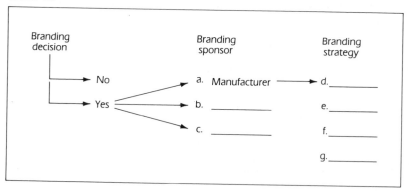

3 Comprehension/interpretation

3.1 What do you think the advantages are of a generic name from the consumer's point of view?

3.2 Why do you think consumers prefer private labels rather than manufacturer labels in the fashion industry?

3.3 Why do you think Procter & Gamble have always used individual names for their household detergents (e.g. Ariel, Tide, Dash and Bold)?

3.4 Do you think the Apple Macintosh is a good name for a computer? If so, why?

4 Language focus

4.1 Question formation: **wh-** questions (see Unit 38 in *Language Reference for Business English*)

Look at the following sentences taken from the Reading passage:

'*Why* have branding in the first place?'
'*Who* benefits from branding?'

You are trying to identify brand preference by asking shoppers questions in a supermarket. Now ask about the following:

1. Frequency of shopping visits.
2. Reason for shopping visits.
3. Person in the household who generally does the shopping.
4. Types of purchases in the supermarket.
5. Budget for weekly shop.
6. Preference for branded products.
7. Types of branded products purchased.
8. Price premium prepared to pay.
9. Knowledge of the product – name, etc.
10. Satisfaction with branded products.

4.2   Question formation: **yes/no** questions (see Unit 38 in *Language Reference for Business English*)

Look at the following sentences taken from the Reading passage:

> '*Do we launch* it under the manufacturer's own label?'
> '*Should we combine* these two strategies . . . ?'

Now ask consumers questions about their buying behaviour:

1. Ask if s/he enjoys shopping.
2. Ask if s/he shops in large supermarkets.
3. Ask if s/he thinks shopping services have improved.
4. Ask if s/he spends about three hours shopping a week.
5. Ask if s/he uses a mint toothpaste.
6. Ask if s/he has heard of Dentigum.
7. Ask if s/he has tried Dentigum.
8. Ask if s/he would like to try a sample.
9. Ask if s/he liked the sample.
10. Ask if s/he would like to buy some.

5 Word study

Match the words with their definitions:

Words	Definitions
1. Brand	a. is a brand or part of a brand that is given legal protection
2. Brand name	b. is the exclusive legal right to reproduce, publish or sell the matter
3. Brand mark	c. is a name, term, sign, symbol, or a design or a combination of them intended to identify the goods or services
4. Trade mark	d. is that part of the brand which can be recognised but is not utterable, such as a symbol, design, colouring or lettering
5. Copyright	e. is that part of a brand that can be vocalised – is utterable

6 Transfer

PAIR WORK (Partner B turn to the Key section)

A: Use Chart 4.2 to ask questions about a new men's toiletry. Together you should
come to a decision about branding this product.

Product	Anti-wrinkle cream for men
Core product – benefits	
Tangible product – features package quality branding	
Manufacturer	

Part 2: Product line decisions

1 Warm-up

1.1   What are the dangers of being a one-product company?

1.2   What are the dangers of over-extending a company's product spread?

2 Listening

Listen to the presentation given by the managing director of the training organisation. As you listen, complete Charts 4.3 to 4.6.

Chart 4.3   Product mix

Language training	a. _____	b. _____

Chart 4.4   Product lines

English French a. _____ b. _____ c. _____	Presentation skills d. _____ e. _____	Leadership skills f. _____ g. _____

Chart 4.5   Product depth

Group Individual English training	a. _____ b. _____ Presentation skills	c. _____ Leadership skills

Chart 4.6 Product developments

a. Product mix   +   _____
b. Product line   +   _____
c. Product depth   +   _____

3 Comprehension/interpretation

3.1 What is the difference between a public and a company seminar?

3.2 Do you think information technology training would be consistent with their existing product mix?

3.3 Which of the potential product development areas (mix, line or depth) would be the most risky?

4 Language focus

4.1 Past reference (see Unit 63 in *Language Reference for Business English*)

Look at the following sentences taken from the Listening passage:

'We started *back in 1980* . . .'
'The language training has developed *over the years* . . .'

Now complete the following sentences with one of the time 'prepositions' below:

over   ago   on   in   at   since   for

1. He's been off work _____ three months.
2. He ought to have retired a year _____.
3. She's been with the company _____ it began.
4. It's hard to gauge success _____ just two months.
5. She left the country _____ 1400 _____ Tuesday.
6. We didn't receive the delivery _____ time.
7. _____ the beginning of the year, prospects looked good.
8. There was a downturn _____ the middle of March.
9. _____ 1980, our prices have been falling.
10. We installed a new computer network two years _____ .

4.2 Scale of likelihood (see Unit 80 in *Language Reference for Business English*)

Look at the following sentences taken from the Listening passage:

'A second area *might* be to stretch one of the product lines . . .'
'Alternatively, we *could* focus on some of our more profitable training areas . . .'

Now match the expressions:

1. It's certain	a. We're likely to survive
2. It's probable	b. We could develop a new product
3. It's possible	c. We can't survive
4. It's just possible	d. We will develop a new product
5. It's improbable	e. We should reach 20,000
6. It's impossible	f. There's a slight chance of success
	g. We're unlikely to reach 40,000
	h. We might go bankrupt
	i. There's no chance of surviving

5 Word study

Many verbs have derivative forms (noun, adjectives, etc.). For example:

to produce   a product, production, productive, productivity

Complete the sentences below by inserting the right derivative of the verbs in brackets:

5.1   The contract is not _____ . (to negotiate)
5.2   We did a very _____ survey of consumer behaviour. (to extend)
5.3   We need to assess the _____ qualities of our new managers. (to lead)
5.4   There is a _____ between product mix and product depth. (to distinguish)
5.5   He gave a _____ about the company's performance. (to present)
5.6   To increase _____ , we have offered _____ bonuses to the employees. (to produce)
5.7   Before we can decide about developing new products, we need to know how _____ the existing products are. (to profit)
5.8   He's one of the best _____ I've met. (to negotiate)

6 Transfer

Use the information in Charts 4.3 to 4.6 to write a brief report on the training organisation's product profile and development potential.

Section B: Product development decisions

Part 1: New product development

1 Warm-up

1.1 What do you think is the success rate of new products?
1.2 Why do you think so many new products fail?

2 Reading

Read the article below about new product development. As you read it, complete Chart 4.7.

The average cost of developing and introducing a major new product from scratch has jumped to well over $100 million. To make things worse, many of these costly new products fail (some sources estimate that 80 per cent of all new products introduced in the United States fail). So companies are now pursuing new product strategies that are less costly and risky than developing completely new brands. Here we describe three new product strategies: acquiring new brands, developing 'me-too' products, and reviving old brands.

Acquiring new products
Instead of building its own new products from the ground up, a company can buy another company and its established brands. The mid-1980s saw a dramatic flurry of one big company gobbling up another. Procter & Gamble acquired Richardson-Vicks, Thomson Electronics bought RCA, Nestlé absorbed Rowntree Mackintosh, Philip Morris obtained General Foods, and Schweppes merged with Cadbury.

Such acquisitions can be tricky – the company must be certain that the acquired products blend with its current products and that the firm has the skills and resources needed to continue to run the acquired brands profitably. Acquisitions can run into snags with government regulators. For example, even under the Reagan Administrations' loose antitrust policy, regulators did not allow Pepsi to acquire 7-Up. Finally, such acquisitions have high price tags. Philip Morris coughed up $5.7 billion for General Foods and Nestlé forked out over $2.5 billion for Rowntree Mackintosh. But despite high initial outlays, buying established brands may be cheaper in the long run than paying the enormous costs of trying to create well-known brands from scratch. Moreover, acquiring proven winners eliminates almost all the risks of new-product failure. Acquisitions also provides a quick and easy way to gain access to new markets or strengthen positions in current markets.

Developing 'me-too' products
In recent years, many companies have used 'me-too' product strategies – introducing imitations of successful competing products. Thus Tandy, Sanyo, Compaq and many

others produce IBM-compatible personal computers. These 'clones' sometimes sell for less than half the price of the IBM models they emulate. Imitation is now fair play for products ranging from soft drinks to toiletries.

Me-too products are often quicker and less expensive to develop. The market-leader pioneers the technology and bears most of the product development costs while the imitative product can sometimes offer more value than the market-leading originals. Furthermore, me-too products are less costly and risky to introduce – they enter a proven market, riding on the coattails of the market-leader.

On the other hand, a me-too strategy has some drawbacks. The imitating company enters the market late and must battle a successful, firmly entrenched competitor.

Reviving old products

Many companies have found 'new gold in the old' by reviving once-successful brands that are now dead or dying. Many old and tarnished brand names still hold magic for consumers. Often, simply reviving, reformulating and repositioning an old brand can give the company a successful 'new' product at a fraction of the cost of building new brands.

There are some classic examples of brand revivals. Ivory Soap reversed its sales decline in the early 1970s when it was repromoted for adult use rather than just for babies. Dannon yogurt sales rocketed as a result of linking it to healthy living. Warner-Lambert revived Black Jack gum by playing on the nostalgia of its 110-year old name; Coca-Cola rejuvenated Fresca by adding NutraSweet and real fruit juices.

Sometimes a dead product rises again with a new name as happened with one of Nestlé's cookery brands. Some years ago Nestlé withdrew a product when it failed in test market, but later revived the line under the Lean Cuisine brand to fit with today's health-conscious consumers.

Nevertheless, there are dangers with reviving old brands. Perhaps the biggest of them is that it can encourage marketers to look back rather than forwards.

Chart 4.7

Strategies	Examples	Advantages	Disadvantages
Acquisition			
Me-toos			
Revivals			

3 Comprehension/interpretation

3.1   Why do government regulators sometimes prevent an acquisition from taking place?

3.2   Can you think of any other examples of successful me-too products?

3.3   Why did Nestlé relaunch their cookery product?

4 Language focus

4.1   Connectors 1 (see Units 67 and 72 in *Language Reference for Business English*)

Look at the following sentences taken from the Reading passage:

> '*But despite* high initial outlays, buying established brands may be cheaper . . .'
> '*Moreover*, acquiring proven winners eliminates almost all the risks . . .'

Now select connectors from the list below to complete the sentences:

however   **moreover**   **despite**   **thus**   **in addition**   **although**

1. _____ investing nearly $20m in the project, they soon ran out of funds.
2. _____ profits are high at the moment, we must expect a downturn next year.
3. They acquired two US companies in 1989. _____ , they bought several smaller European enterprises in the same year.
4. The company developed a very good me-too product. _____, they found it impossible to break into the market.
5. They developed an IBM clone and _____ broke into the lucrative PC market.
6. There have been many successful revivals. _____ these products have also saved their companies a considerable amount in product development costs.

4.2   Connectors 2 (see Units 67 and 72 in *Language Reference for Business English*)

Look at the following sentence taken from the Reading passage:

> 'The market-leader pioneers the technology *while* the imitative product offers more value . . .'

Combine these pairs of sentences with an appropriate connector:

1. Sales have decreased.
   Profits have increased.
2. One advantage is that you have instant access to the market.
   You can deliberately undercut your competitors.
3. We were making a loss.
   We withdrew from the market.
4. The product sold well in the South.
   In the North, the results were disastrous.
5. We promoted the product at the point of sale.
   Our competitors used mass advertising.

5 Word study

Complete the boxes by choosing appropriate words/expressions from the list below:

to succeed	dead	to move into	to gobble up	to cough up
tarnished	to merge	to pay out	to strengthen your	to rise
to reverse the	to fork out	to rejuvenate	hold	again
decline	to obtain	to enter	to ride on the	to rocket
to absorb	to take over	dying	coattails	to revive

Success	Old products	Market penetration
_____	_____	_____
_____	_____	_____
_____	_____	_____
	_____	_____
	_____	
	_____	

Acquisition	Payment	
_____	_____	
_____	_____	
_____	_____	
_____		

6 Transfer

Using Chart 4.7 and the expressions above, present the alternative product development strategies for your company or a typical business.

Part 2: Product life cycle

1 Warm-up

Once a product has reached its maximum sales level in a given sector, what strategies can be used to extend its life and profitability for as long as possible?

2 Listening

Listen to the product manager present the sales and profits achieved by her product. As you listen, complete Chart 4.8.

Chart 4.8

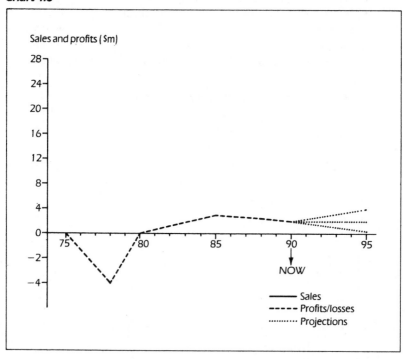

3 Comprehension/interpretation

3.1 How does the product manager divide her presentation?
3.2 Why did the company make a loss of $4 million in 1978?
3.3 Why did profits decline in the period 1985 to 1988.
3.4 What does she mean by a premium price for the AZ1000?

4 Language focus

4.1 Describing graphs (see Unit 68 in *Language Reference for Business English*)

Look at the following sentence taken from the Listening passage:

'The *dotted lines representing a projection* . . .'

Now match the letters (a–g) with the terms used to describe graphs (1–7):

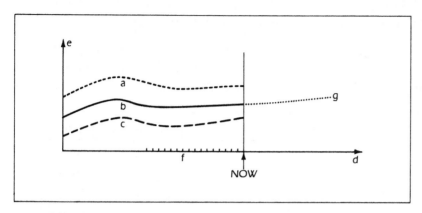

1. solid line
2. broken line
3. a horizontal axis
4. a scale
5. a projection
6. a vertical axis
7. a dotted line

4.2 Describing trends (see Unit 68 in *Language Reference for Business English*)

Look at the following sentences taken from the Listening passage:

'Sales began to *climb* . . .'
'Our investment costs *reached their peak* . . .'

Now match the phrases used to describe trends (1–10) with points marked on the graph (a–j):

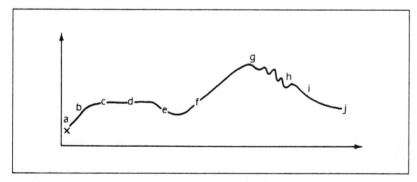

1. reached a peak
2. fluctuated wildly
3. rose sharply
4. flattened out
5. plateaued
6. remained constant
7. recovered
8. decreased steadily
9. stood at
10. dipped

5 Word study

Complete the table by inserting the words from the list below:

Product awareness   Laggards   Peak levels   Defend share
Few   Improved   Slow growth   Many rivals
Negative   Falling   Rising

	Introduction	Growth	Maturity	Decline
Characteristics				
Sales	Low	Fast growth	a. _____	Decline
Profits	Negligible	b. _____	Declining	Low/zero
Cash flow	c. _____	Moderate	High	Low
Customers	Innovative	Mass-market	Mass market	d. _____
Competitors	e. _____	Increasing	f. _____	Declining
Responses				
Strategic focus	Expand market	Market penetration	g. _____	Productivity
Marketing expenditure	High	High	h. _____	Low
Marketing emphasis	i. _____	Brand preference	Brand loyalty	Selective
Distribution	Patchy	Intensive	Intensive	Selective
Price	High	Lower	Lowest	j. _____
Product	Basic	k. _____	Differentiated	Unchanged

6 Transfer

Use Chart 4.8 (product life cycle) and the language above to write a summary of product growth and potential.

UNIT 5
Pricing

Price is all around us. You pay *rent* for your apartment, *tuition* for your education, and a *fee* to your doctor or dentist. The airline, taxi and bus companies charge you a *fare*, the local services call their price a *rate;* and the local bank makes you pay *charges* and *interest* for the money you borrow. The price for driving your car on a motorway is a *toll* and the company that insures you charges a *premium.* The guest speaker charges you an *honorarium* to tell you about the government official who took a *bribe* to help some character steal *dues* collected by the trade union. Your regular lawyer may ask for a *retainer* to cover his/her services. The price of an executive is a *salary*, the price of a salesperson may be a *commission,* and the price of a worker is a *wage.*

Section A: Factors to consider when setting prices

Part 1: Analysis of price–demand relationship

1 *Warm-up*

1.1   Does a lower price always mean higher sales?
1.2   For what types of product do higher prices sometimes mean higher sales?

2 *Reading*

Read the following extract about the price-demand relationship. As you read, label Charts 5.1 a–f as referred to in the text.

Each price the company might charge will lead to a different level of demand. The relation between the price charged and the resulting demand level is shown in the familiar demand curve in Figure 5.1. This curve shows that the higher the price, the lower the demand. Thus the company will sell less if it raises its prices.

Most demand curves slope downwards in either a straight or curved line as in Figure 5.1. But for prestige goods, the demand curve sometimes slopes upwards as in Figure 5.2. In this case, if a company raises its price from P_1 to P_2 it will actually sell more rather than less. However, if the company charges too high a price (P_3), the level of demand will be lower than P_2.

Most companies try to measure their demand curves. To do this, they need to estimate demand at different prices. Figure 5.3 shows the estimated demand curve for a motor oil product. Demand rises as the price is lowered but then suddenly drops at around 40 cents, possibly due to consumers thinking the oil is too cheap and might damage their cars.

Economists show the impact of non-price factors on demand through shifts of the demand curve, rather than movements along the curve. Suppose the initial demand curve is D_1 in Figure 5.4. The seller is charging P and selling Q_1 units. Now suppose the economy suddenly improves or the seller doubles its advertising budget. This causes an increase in demand shown by the upward shift of the demand curve from D_1 to D_2. Without changing the price P, the sellers demand is now Q_2.

Marketers need to know price elasticity or how responsive demand will be to a change in price. In Figure 5.5 a price increase from P_1 to P_2 leads to a relatively small drop in demand from Q_1 to Q_2. In Figure 5.6 the same price increase results in a large drop in demand. If demand hardly changes with a change in price, we say the demand is *inelastic*. If demand changes a lot, we say the demand is *elastic*. The price elasticity of demand is given by the following formula:

$$\text{price elasticity of demand} = \frac{\%\ \text{change in quantity demanded}}{\%\ \text{change in price}}$$

Say demand falls by 10 per cent when the retailer raises its price by 2 per cent. Price elasticity of demand is therefore 5 and demand is elastic. If demand falls by 2 per cent with a 2 per cent increase in price, then elasticity is 1. In this case, the seller sells fewer items but at a higher price, which therefore preserves the same total revenue.

If demand falls by 1 per cent when the price is increased by 2 per cent, then elasticity is ½ and demand is inelastic. The less elastic the demand, the more profitable it is for the seller to raise the price.

If demand is elastic rather than inelastic, sellers will consider lowering their price. A lower price will produce more total revenue. This strategy works as long as the extra costs of producing and selling do not exceed the extra revenue.

Chart 5.1

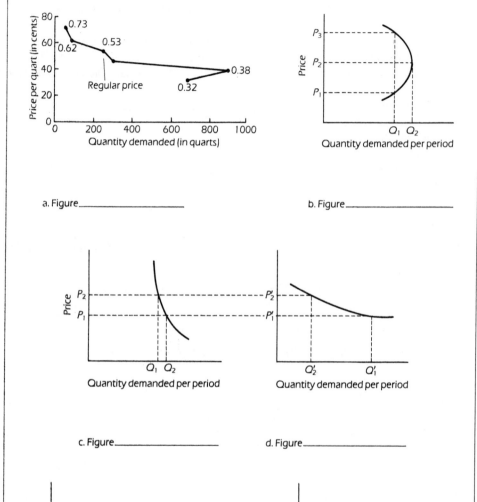

a. Figure_____

b. Figure_____

c. Figure_____

d. Figure_____

e. Figure_____

f. Figure_____

3 Comprehension/interpretation

Now give a title to each of the figures above. Choose from the following:

Inelastic demand   Demand curve for motor oil
Elastic demand   Standard demand curve
Prestige goods demand curve Effect of non-price factors on demand

3.1 Figure 5.1: _____
3.2 Figure 5.2: _____
3.3 Figure 5.3: _____
3.4 Figure 5.4: _____
3.5 Figure 5.5: _____
3.6 Figure 5.6: _____

4 Language focus

4.1 Cause and effect – verbs (see Unit 77 in *Language Reference for Business English*)

Look at the following sentences taken from the Reading passage:

> 'Each price the company might charge will *lead to* a different level of demand.'
> 'The same price increase *results in* a large drop in demand.'

Now match cause with effect to complete the sentences below:

Cause	Effect
price increase	staff motivation falls
sales decrease	fall in demand
advertising doubled	redundancies
market sector decline	sales increase
salaries reduction	share price drop

1. Price increases can _____ to _____ .
2. A sales decrease may _____ in _____ .
3. Doubling of the advertising budget should _____ to _____ .
4. A gradual decline in the market sector has _____ in _____ .
5. A reduction in staff salaries will _____ to _____ .

4.2 Cause and effect – if clauses, etc. (see Unit 77 in *Language Reference for Business English*)

Look at the following sentences taken from the Reading passage:

> '*If* a company *raises* its price, it *will* actually *sell* more . . .'
> 'The *less* elastic the demand, the *more* profitable *it is* for the seller to raise the price.'

Now use the vicious circle (spiral) below to complete the sentences:

Cause	Effect
companies raise wages	production costs increase
production costs increase	prices rise
prices rise	demand falls
demand falls	sales decrease
sales decrease	production falls

1. If the company raises wages, _____
2. The more the production costs increase, _____
3. If prices rise _____
4. The more demand falls, _____
5. If sales decrease, _____

5 Word study

Match the price term with the person or organisation that charges it:

Price term	Person/organisation charging
1. salary	a. visiting lecturer
2. rate	b. insurance company
3. premium	c. white-collar worker
4. fare	d. local council
5. commission	e. social club
6. fee	f. blue-collar worker
7. rent	g. taxi driver
8. dues	h. sales agent
9. retainer	i. private school
10. tuition	j. lawyer
11. wage	k. bridge owner
12. toll	l. bank
13. honorarium	m. architect
14. interest	n. property owner

6 Transfer

Study Charts 5.2 and 5.3 on the next page. Use them as a basis to present your decision for pricing the new men's toiletry – anti-wrinkle cream.

Chart 5.2   Women's anti-wrinkle cream

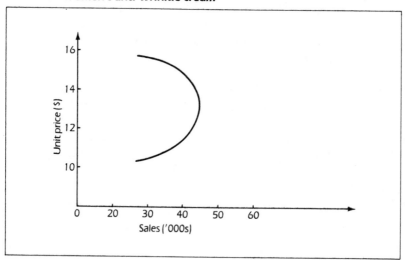

Chart 5.3   Effect of advertising

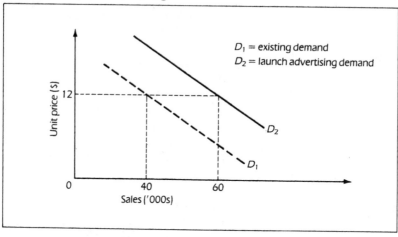

D_1 = existing demand
D_2 = launch advertising demand

Part 2: Pricing decisions

1 *Warm-up*

1.1   What do you think are the typical 'mark-ups' on manufacturers' prices for:

   - tobacco products
   - bakery products
   - greeting cards
   - perfumes

1.2   How does a retailer decide on the appropriate mark-up?

2 Listening

Listen to the internal meeting about pricing. As you listen, complete Chart 5.4.

Chart 5.4

Optimum demand price	Sales at this price	Variable cost	Fixed cost	Retailer mark-up	Manufacturing margin	Going rates
a. _____	b. _____	c. _____	d. _____	e. _____	f. _____	g. _____

3 Comprehension/interpretation

3.1 What is another way of explaining *going rate*?
3.2 What is the formula for calculating manufacturer's costs?
3.3 How do consumers perceive Apollo?
3.4 What is the objective of their targets?

4 Language focus

4.1 Asking for clarification (see Unit 73 in *Language Reference for Business English*)

Look at the following sentences taken from the Listening passage:

'*Excuse me, what do you mean by* going rate?'
'*I'm sorry, can you go over that again?*'

Now complete the following dialogue with appropriate expressions:

A: The central problem is cannibalism.
B: _____ cannibalism?
A: Well, basically our new product taking sales away from our existing product.
_____?
B: Yes, I see what you _____ .
A: Now we have to weigh up the added sales and margin we gain and balance that against our losses.
B: _____ slowly?
A: Of course. Well in order to calculate the real profit we gain from the launch of the ZX21 we must take into account the lost sales on the ZX20.
B: _____
A: Good, now this model here plots the projected sales of the ZX21 over the first twelve months against the projected continued sales of the ZX20. As you can see, the gap widens quite dramatically.
A: If I _____, you're _____ this gap represents lost sales?
B: No, it's not quite that simple.

4.2 Confirming and correcting statements (see Unit 73 in *Language Reference for Business English*)

Look at the following sentences taken from the Listening passage:

> *'That's right.'*
> *'Correct me if I'm wrong? . . . No, that's absolutely right.'*

Now study the figures in Chart 5.5 and then respond appropriately to the sentences below:

Chart 5.5

Price	Expected sales	Estimated profits
£20	22,000	£100,000
£19	24,000	£100,000
£18	25,000	£ 95,000
£17	26,000	£ 90,000

1. So at £20, we can expect profits of £100,000.
2. At a unit price of £19, we can presumably expect higher sales.
3. I suppose we can also expect appreciably higher profits.
4. So, if I understand you, you're saying profits decrease as the price goes down!
5. So there's no benefit in charging a lower price?
6. Correct me if I'm wrong, these figures argue for a price of around £18?

5 Word study

Listen to the numbers/calculations on the cassette and write them down (you should find ten). When you have done this, practise saying the expressions.

6 Transfer

Use Chart 5.5 to present a summary of the pricing discussion and then draw your own conclusions and make recommendations for the pricing of this product.

Section B: Pricing strategies

Part 1: Price wars

1 Warm-up

1.1 How can price be used as an active market penetration strategy?
1.2 Will new competitors always enter the market with lower prices?

2 Reading

Read the extract about a price war in the construction equipment market. As you read it, complete Chart 5.6 using the labels listed at the end.

Caterpillar, Inc., the world's leading maker of heavy construction and mining equipment, has been locked in a long price war with Japanese challenger Komatsu Ltd. In this bloody battle, both companies are using price to buy long-run market share, even if it means lower profits or even losses in the short run. For over fifty years, Caterpillar has dominated the world market for giant construction equipment. It built its 40% market share by emphasising high product quality, dependable after-sales service and a strong dealer body. It used a premium pricing strategy – making high profit margins by convincing buyers that Cat's higher quality and trouble-free operation provided greater value and justified a higher price.

But all this began to change when Komatsu entered the market. The Japanese firm started cautiously in the United States with only a few products. It realised the importance of non-price factors in the buyer's purchase decision. Like Caterpillar, Komatsu stressed high quality and it expanded slowly to allow its parts and service capacity to keep up with sales. But Komatsu's major weapon for taking share from Caterpillar was price. A strong dollar and lower manufacturing costs allowed Komatsu to cut prices ruthlessly – its initial prices were as much as 40% lower than Caterpillar's. On a giant dump truck sold by Cat for $500,000, that could mean a saving of up to $200,000. Riding its strong price advantage, Komatsu grabbed a 17% market share by 1986.

Caterpillar fought back to protect its number one market position and the price war was on. To support lower prices, Cat reduced its workforce by a third and slashed costs by 22%. It vowed to meet Komatsu's prices and in some cases even initiated price cutting. With heavy discounting by both companies, manufacturer's list prices became meaningless. For example, a bulldozer that listed for $140,000 regularly sold for $110,000. In the battle for market share, all competitors lost out on profits, lesser companies were driven to the brink of ruin. Caterpillar lost $1 billion in less than five years and Komatsu, even with its cost advantages, saw its profit decline by 30%.

By 1988, thanks to a falling dollar and its cost-cutting programmes, Caterpillar had managed to regain a quarter of Komatsu's US market share. With a weaker dollar eating into Komatsu's price advantage, the challenger recently raised its prices 5 to 10%. Though fierce price competition continues, Komatsu may be signalling that it wants an end to the fighting and a return to peaceful coexistence and better profits for both companies. It hopes that Caterpillar will respond by raising its prices too.

Chart 5.6

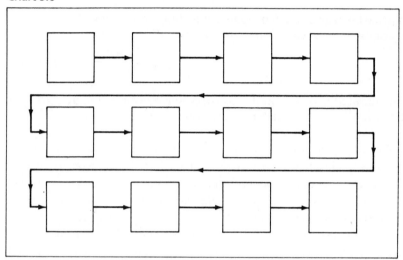

Insert the following actions and responses into the right order in Chart 5.6:

a. competitor enters market
b. profits drastically reduced
c. market leader charges premium prices
d. smaller competitors drop out of market
e. market leader regains market share
f. market leader loses market share
g. market leader holds dominant position
h. competitor undercuts prices dramatically
i. market leader responds by raising prices
j. competitor raises prices
k. market leader responds by cutting costs and prices
l. profit margins restored.

3 Comprehension/interpretation

3.1 What was Komatsu's marketing objective?
3.2 Why was Komatsu able to charge lower prices?
3.3 Did Caterpillar regain its full market share by 1988?
3.4 Why did Komatsu recently have to raise its prices?

4 Language focus

4.1 Past simple (irregular verbs) (see Unit 3 in *Language Reference for Business English*)

Look at the following sentences taken from the Reading passage:

'It *built* its 40% market share by emphasising . . .'
'All this *began* to change when Komatsu entered the market.'

Now put the following sentences into the past:

1. We are fighting off the challenge from our competitors.
2. We have cut prices dramatically.
3. They are outselling us in all sectors of the market.
4. We may lose our dominant position.
5. We have seen a gradual erosion of our position.
6. Komatsu is eating into our share of the market.
7. We are bringing forward our monthly meeting.
8. They are buying into the company by acquiring ordinary shares.
9. We will take market share from our competitors.
10. The whole market has swollen significantly.

4.2 Subordinate clauses (see Unit 44 in *Language Reference for Business English*)

Look at the following sentences taken from the Reading passage:

'Komatsu, *even with its cost advantages*, saw its profits decline by 30%.'
'By 1988, *thanks to a falling dollar and its cost-cutting programmes*, Caterpillar had managed to regain a quarter of Komatsu's US market shares.'

Now make sentences which combine the following information:

1. Caterpillar / reduced prices dramatically / regained market share
2. Komatsu / a low-price strategy / entered the market
3. Construction equipment market / dominated by Caterpillar for many years / now fragmented
4. Prices fell / heavy discounting in the sector / profit margins narrowed
5. Smaller competitors / margins squeezed / forced out of the market
6. Price / a major factor in some markets / ignored in this market

5 Word study

5.1 Raise and rise
These two verbs are often confused. Study this example of how they are used:

a. Komatsu raised its prices   (transitive – with object)
b. Prices rose   (intransitive – no object)

In (a) there is a (grammatical) agent (Komatsu) actively doing something, and there is an object for the verb (prices).

In (b) there is no agent, and there can be no object.

Decide which verb to use in the following sentences:

1. The sun _____ every morning.
2. He _____ the question of salary.
3. Profits _____ last year by 25 per cent.
4. The company was forced to _____ prices.
5. Inflation _____ by 9 per cent this year.

5.2 The Reading extract above uses many words and expressions associated with 'war': for example, *locked in a war*. Go through the extract picking out these words and expressions. You should find a further eight.

6 *Transfer*

Look back at the flowchart (Chart 5.6). Use this as a basis to present the likely development in a price war.

Part 2: Price adjustment strategies

1 *Warm-up*

What sort of price adjustments can be offered to a customer in order to persuade him/her to buy for the first time or to remain loyal to a certain supplier?

2 *Listening*

Listen to the telephone call between a customer and his supplier. As you listen, complete Chart 5.7.

Chart 5.7

Unit price	Quantity discount 200+ 500+		Early payment discount	Promotional allowance
a. _____	b. _____	c. _____	d. _____	e. _____

3 Comprehension/interpretation

Listen again and complete Chart 5.8.

Chart 5.8

Name of caller	Name of called	Reason for call	Follow-up action
a. _____	b. _____	c. _____	d. _____

4 Language focus

4.1   Telephoning (see Skill 3 in *Language Reference for Business English*)

Look at the following sentences taken from the Listening passage:

'*Could you put me through to* Mr Stevens?'
'*The reason I'm phoning is . . .*'

Now put the following telephone call in the right order. The conversation is among the following three people:

　　A – the receptionist at Rogers Electronics
　　B – Max Roberts of Excel Marketing
　　C – Mr Dickens, sales dept, Rogers Electronics

A: I'm sorry I didn't catch your name.
C: You're welcome. Bye.
B: Certainly, perhaps you could give me his extension number?
A: Rogers Electronics.
B: Yes, I'll hang on.
C: Just a moment Mr Roberts. I'll put you on to our Market Research assistant . . . I'm sorry, he's out at the moment, would you like to call back.
B: Good afternoon. this is Max Roberts from Excel Marketing. Could you put me through to your Sales Department?
C: Yes, it's 453. His name is Holden. John Holden.
A: Thank you Mr Roberts. I'll try to put you through . . . I'm afraid the line's busy at the moment. Will you hold?
B: Hello, my name's Max Roberts. I'm from Excel Marketing. The reason I'm calling is that we are carrying out a market survey . . .
C: Sales. Dickens speaking.
B: Goodbye.
A: Right, Mr Roberts. I'm putting you through.
B: It's Roberts.
B: Thanks for your help.

4.2 Offering and requesting (see Unit 82 in *Language Reference for Business English*)

Look at the following sentences taken from the Listening passage:

> *'We were wondering what sort of quantity discount you can offer us.'*
> *'We would be willing to offer you a 10 per cent discount.'*

Now soften the following dialogue:

A: We want a discount.
B: Okay, we can discuss it.
A: What can you offer?
B: What about 2 per cent?
A: You must be joking.
B: No, I'm serious.
A: Surely you can do better than that.
B: Maybe another ½ per cent.
A: We wanted 5 per cent.
B: That's out of the question.
A: What about 3½ per cent?
B: That's far too high.
A: We can always go elsewhere, you know?
B: I know that. Perhaps we can settle on 3 per cent.
A: I accept that.
B: Good. We'll leave it at that then.

5 Word study

Complete the table opposite by selecting from the following words/expressions (a–j):

a. not the end user
b. purchasing large quantities
c. improves cash flow
d. encourages sales in slow selling periods
e. encourages sales in new lines
f. purchased out of season
g. participation in sales promotion
h. saves on inventory and distribution costs
i. middlemen cover some sales and distribution functions
j. prompt or early payment

Type of price adjustment	Condition	Reason
1. Cash discount		
2. Quantity discount		
3. Trade discount		
4. Seasonal discount		
5. Promotional allowance		

6 Transfer

PAIR WORK (**Partner B turn to the Key section**)

A: **You are the purchaser. You are planning to buy hairdryers to sell to your retail outlets. You are planning to purchase between 200 and 300 hairdryers per month. You have been quoted a unit price of £10 per hairdryer. Telephone the supplier (B) and negotiate as much discount as possible.**

UNIT 6
Placing

Section A: Distribution channels

Part 1: Distribution channels: types and organisation

1 Warm-up

1.1 Why do manufacturers use middlemen rather than selling directly to their end customers?

1.2 What are the dangers of using middlemen rather than selling direct?

2 Reading

Read the extract about *vertical marketing systems.* As you read it, complete the tree diagram in Chart 6.1.

> In recent years, one of the biggest channel developments has been the vertical marketing systems (VMS) that have emerged to challenge conventional marketing channels. Generally they provide stronger leadership and improved performance.
>
> In contrast to the conventional distribution channel, VMS consists of producers, and wholesalers acting as a unified system. Any of these three channel members can own, have contracts with or have influence over the other two members. VMS achieve economies through size, bargaining power and elimination of duplicated services. We will now look at the three major types of VMS shown in Chart 6.1.

Chart 6.1

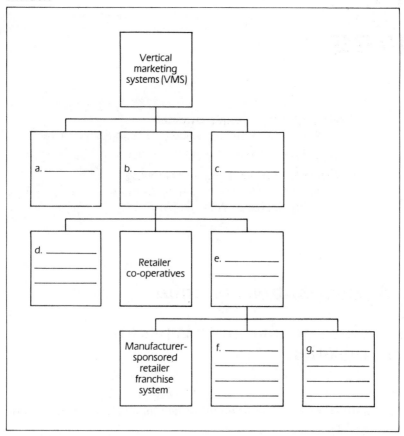

Each type uses a different means for setting up leadership and power in the channel.

In a *corporate VMS* the many stages of production and distribution are combined under single ownership. For example, Gallo, the world's largest wine maker, does much more than simply turn grapes into wine. The Gallo brothers own the trucking company which transports all the wine out of Modesto and many of the raw materials back in. Gallo makes the bottles and the aluminium screw tops. It participates in every aspect of selling and owns its distributors in about twelve markets and would probably buy many more if the laws in a lot of states did not prohibit it from doing so.

A *contractual VMS* consists of independent firms at different levels of production and distribution who join together through contracts to obtain more economies or sales than they could achieve alone. There are three types of contractual VMS: *wholesaler-sponsored voluntary chains, retailer co-operatives* and *franchise organisations*.

Wholesaler-sponsored voluntary chains are systems in which wholesalers organise voluntary chains of independent retailers to help them compete with large chain organisations. This is quite common amongst independent grocers.

Retailer cooperatives are systems in which retailers organise a new, jointly-owned business to carry out wholesaling and possibly even production.

In franchise organisations, a channel member called a *franchiser* might link several stages in the production-distribution process. There are three forms of franchises. The *manufacturer-sponsored retailer franchise* system is common in the automobile industry. The manufacturer licenses independent dealers to sell its cars. The *manufacturer-sponsored wholesale franchise* is found in the soft-drink industry. Coca-Cola, for example, licenses bottlers (wholesalers) in some markets. They buy the manufacturer's syrup concentrate and then carbonate, bottle and sell it to retailers in local markets. The third franchise form is the *service firm-sponsored retailer franchise* system. Here a service firm organises a whole system for bringing its service to consumers. There are many examples including car rental (Hertz, Avis), fast-food (McDonalds, Burger King) and the motel business (Holiday Inn, Ramada Inn).

Finally, an *administered VMS* coordinates the many stages of production and distribution not through common ownership or contractual ties but through the size and power of one of the parties. Manufacturers of top brands can obtain strong trade co-operation. Thus Procter & Gamble or Campbell Soups can command a lot of cooperation from resellers regarding shelf-space, displays, promotions and price policies.

3 Comprehension/interpretation

3.1 What are the advantages of VMS over conventional distribution channels?

3.2 What are the advantages of:
   (i) Wholesale sponsored chains?
   (ii) Retail co-operatives?
   (iii) Franchise organisations?

3.3 Which party in an administered VMS is most likely to be the leader?

4 Language focus

4.1 Quantity and amount (see Unit 59 in *Language Reference for Business English*)

Look at the following sentences taken from the Reading passage:

'*Any* of these three channel members can own, have contacts with . . .'
'*Each* type uses a different means . . .'

Now complete the sentences by inserting one of the following:

   all   any   each   every

1. We sell _____ type you like.
2. We are involved in _____ the stages of wine production and distribution.
3. We have studied _____ step in the distribution process.

---

4. We studied _____ of the major wine producers. _____ of them has some advantage.
5. You asked me if we can supply _____ retailer in the north of England. In fact, we can reach _____ one within a thirty mile radius of Newcastle.
6. We are involved in _____ aspect of wine distribution.
7. _____ major wine producers have suffered from the recession.

4.2 Noun compounds (see Unit 46 in *Language Reference for Business English*)

Look at the following sentences taken from the Reading passage:

> 'The *manufacturer-sponsored retailer franchise system* is common in the automobile industry.'
> '*Wholesaler-sponsored voluntary chains* are systems . . .'

Now create noun compounds for the following:

1. A franchise system for retailers which is sponsored by service firms.
2. A distribution network for wholesalers which is funded by manufacturers.
3. A co-operative for customers which is run by retailers.
4. A market survey of competitors which is financed by industry.
5. An association of employers which is supported by the government.
6. A union of employees which is threatened by bankruptcy.

5 *Word study*

Complete the following table:

Activity	Person who offers	Person who receives
employment	employer	employee
franchising	_____	_____
licensing	_____	_____
leasing	_____	_____
_____	vendor	_____

6 *Transfer*

Discuss what you consider the most effective system for the following operations:

- A retail health food business, supplied by a number of wholesalers.
- A chocolate manufacturer, operating nationally, wanting to protect itself and its market from multinationals.

Part 2: Managing channels

1 Warm-up

1.1 What are the advantages/disadvantages of exclusive versus selective agreements with agents?

1.2 What are the best ways to motivate agents to achieve their sales targets?

2 Listening

Listen to the telephone call between a sales manager and one of his agents. As you listen, complete Chart 6.2.

Chart 6.2

Product	Actual results	Target
XR50 XR100 XR120		

3 Comprehension/interpretation

3.1 When did they set the targets?

3.2 Were the targets set by the sales manager alone?

3.3 What is the agent's excuse for not reaching the targets as a whole?

3.4 What is the agent's specific excuse for not reaching the target for the XR100?

3.5 Why is the sales manager pleased with the results on the XR120?

4 Language focus

4.1 Responding positively and negatively (see Skill 6 in *Language Reference for Business English*)

Look at the following responses taken from the Listening passage:

Exactly!
Okay
Yes, well . . .
That's fine
Oh . . . that's rather disappointing.

Now choose the most appropriate response:

1. I'm afraid we're well below target.
   a. Okay
   b. Yes, well
   c. Oh . . . why's that?

2. I'm very pleased with my results.
   a. Exactly
   b. Good
   c. Yes

3. We are way ahead of our targets.
   a. Oh
   b. That's good to hear
   c. Fine

4. I was just 'phoning to see how things are going.
   a. I'm fine
   b. I've been ill
   c. Could be better

5. We've just had a disastrous month.
   a. Really, why's that?
   b. That's not true
   c. Good

6. We're heading for a record year.
   a. I'm very interested
   b. Fine
   c. That's marvellous

4.2 Modifiers/softeners (see Unit 70 in *Language Reference for Business English*)

Look at the following extracts from the Listening passage:

'*In a way*, it has been . . .'
'*Well perhaps* I was *a bit* over-optimistic.'
'It's *just* a question of giving up more time.'

Insert one or two of the following words/phrases in order to modify/soften the sentences below:

just   perhaps   a bit   in a way

1. He's too ambitious.
2. Let's go through your figures.
3. We're growing too fast.
4. He's much too direct.
5. We are a little late.
6. Your products are expensive.
7. I'm unsure of your liquidity.
8. That's not good enough.

5 Word study

TARGETS

to fix/set a target

to be | ambitious
| (over-)optimistic
| realistic
| pessimistic

to reach/hit/achieve a target

to be | just a little | above target
| just about | on target
| way | below target

Look at these figures and then complete the sentences below:

Products	Actual results	Target
Apollo	245,000 units	250,000 units
Artemis	149,000 units	150,000 units
Diane	240,000 units	190,000 units

1. We were _____ with the Apollo line.
2. We were _____ with the Artemis line.
3. We were _____ with the Diane lines.

Perhaps we can conclude that:

4. We were a little _____ when we _____ the targets for the Apollo line.
5. We were _____ when we _____ the targets for the Artemis line.
6. We were _____ when we _____ the targets for the Diane line.

6 Transfer

Write a short memo re. your agent in Italy (Giorgio), summarising his recent results and making recommendations for action.

Section B: Wholesaling and retailing

Part 1: Wholesaler marketing decisions

1 Warm-up

1.1 In the age of conglomeration and Vertical Marketing Systems, do you think independent wholesalers have a future?

1.2 What services can a wholesaler offer a manufacturer to add value to their basic service?

2 Reading

Read the following extract about wholesaler marketing decisions. As you read it, complete Chart 6.3.

Wholesalers, like retailers, must make decisions on their target market, product assortment, pricing, promotion and place. Many wholesalers make the mistake of serving too many customers. They need to define their target market. They need to identify the more profitable customers and design stronger offers and build relationships with them. On the other hand, they need to discourage the customers who are not profitable enough by requiring larger orders or adding surcharges to smaller ones.

The wholesaler's product is his assortment. Unfortunately, many of them carry too wide a range of goods. They should not carry too many lines or too much stock. They need to identify the more profitable lines and vary inventory levels accordingly.

Wholesalers usually mark up the cost of goods by about 20 per cent to cover their expenses. This often leaves a margin of about 3 per cent profit. Wholesalers are beginning to experiment with new approaches to prices. They are cutting margins on some lines in order to win new customers, and on other lines they are asking for special prices when they can increase the supplier's sales.

Most wholesalers are not promotion-minded enough. Their use of trade advertising, sales promotion, publicity and personal selling is largely haphazard. They need to adopt some of the image-making techniques used by retailers. They certainly need to develop an overall promotion strategy.

Finally, wholesalers typically locate in low-rent, low-tax areas and put very little money into their physical setting and offices. In many cases they don't invest enough in materials-handling and order-processing systems. To meet rising costs, they need to study the advantages of automated handling procedures. Progressive wholesalers have already moved over to the automated warehouse where orders are fed into a computer, items are picked up by mechanical devices and conveyed on a belt to the despatch area for packing. Many wholesalers are now using computers to carry out accounting, billing, inventory control and forecasting.

Chart 6.3

Decision areas	Present characteristics	Needs
Target markets		
Assortment		
Pricing Promotion		
Place		

3 Comprehension/interpretation

3.1 How can wholesalers discourage less profitable customers?
3.2 In what cases might a supplier offer a wholesaler a higher margin?
3.3 Why don't wholesalers invest in their physical setting?
3.4 What are some of the advantages of automated materials handling?

4 Language focus

4.1 Present simple versus present continuous (see Units 1 and 2 in *Language Reference for Business English*)

Look at the following sentences taken from the Reading passage:

'Unfortunately, many of them *carry* too wide a range of goods.'
'They *are cutting* margins on some lines . . .'

Now put the verbs in either present simple or present continuous:

1. Usually we _____ (destock) at this time of year. This year we _____ (stock up).
2. Wholesalers generally _____ (not interested) in their physical location. However, this _____ (change). Some companies _____ (reposition) themselves through promotion and investment.
3. Inventory control _____ (remain) absolutely essential but fewer stock lines _____ (mean) the wholesaler can _____ (direct) his attention more to the commercial side.
4. In my opinion, Excom Distribution _____ (make) a mistake by relocating to outside town.
5. Many wholesalers _____ (make) the mistake of handling too many lines.
6. We _____ (move) our premises in order to reduce transportation costs.
7. If transportation costs _____ (come down), we will be able to invest in automated handling.
8. He always _____ (talk) about investing but he never _____ (do) anything.

4.2 Too/enough (see Unit 52 in *Language Reference for Business English*)

Look at the following sentences taken from the Reading passage:

'Many wholesalers make the mistake of serving *too* many customers.'
'They need to discourage the customers who are *not* profitable *enough* . . .'

Now express the following sentences in another way using either **too** or **enough**. For example:

We're **too** poor. → We're not rich **enough**.

1. That's too cheap.
2. There's not enough investment.
3. There's too little advertising.
4. The accounting system is too complex.
5. We don't use enough automation.
6. We don't promote enough.
7. We're not imaginative enough.

5 *Word study*

Match the verb with an appropriate preposition:

Verbs	Prepositions
1. to put money	
2. to invest	a. with
3. to carry	b. in
4. to locate	c. up
5. to feed	d. out
6. to pick	e. over
7. to move	f. for
8. to experiment	g. into
9. to ask	
10. to mark	
11. to build a relationship	

6 *Transfer*

ROLE-PLAY
Divide the group into three roles (wholesalers, suppliers and customers). Discuss the needs and wants of these three parties in an efficient distribution channel.

Part 2: Order processing

1 Warm-up

1.1 Do you think marketing people should get involved in delivery problems?
1.2 What are some of the classic excuses for late delivery?

2 Listening

Listen to the two telephone calls between a customer and member of the sales department. As you listen, note down the details of the deliveries in Chart 6.4.

Chart 6.4

	Order no.	Product	Quantity	Delivery due	Action
1st order 2nd order	—	—			

3 Comprehension/interpretation

3.1 How did you think the supplier handled these telephone calls?
3.2 How did you think the customer handled these calls?

4 Language focus

4.1 Time prepositions (see Unit 63 in *Language Reference for Business English*)

Look at the following sentences taken from the Listening passage:

'I know our orders are despatched *at* the end of every week.'
'We should be able to get them to you *by* the beginning of next week.'

Now complete the following sentences with one of the prepositions below:

at   in   by   on

1. Your delivery will be with you _____ two weeks, at the latest.
2. We expected delivery _____ the 21st. They are now promising delivery _____ Tuesday.
3. It'll be despatched _____ Tuesday, _____ the earliest.
4. We normally receive your order _____ the beginning of the month and we deliver _____ the middle of the following month.
5. You assured us of delivery _____ the end of the month, if not sooner.
6. We despatched the goods to you _____ the afternoon. They should be with you _____ tomorrow morning.

4.2   Telephoning (see Skill 3 in *Language Reference for Business English*)

Look at the following sentences taken from the Listening passage:

> 'Look, *can I call you back?*'
> 'Right, *I'll phone you back in the next ten minutes.*'

Now reorder the following telephone call between:

A: Geoff Peters, a conference guest
B: Martine Donaugh, a conference organiser

A: Fine, have you got my number?
B: Hello, Mr Peters. This is Martine Donaugh. How can I help you?
A: It's 031-465-389, extension 26.
B: Oh, I am sorry. You haven't received it then?
A: Hello, this is Geoff Peters, I'm phoning about the conference next week.
B: Right, I've got that. I'll call you back in a few minutes. Goodbye.
A: No, and the conference starts tomorrow.
B: I'm sure I have, but just in case, I'll take it again.
A: Well you promised to send me details of travel and accommodation.
B: Of course. Look, can I check the file and call you back?
A: Goodbye.

5 *Word study*

Here are three verbs that are often confused:

to supply   to deliver   to despatch

Check their meaning and usage in a dictionary. Then complete the following sentences with the appropriate form of one of them:

1. He's been our sole _____ of steel for twenty years.
2. We expected _____ by the end of the month.
3. We have asked them to quote for _____ 20 units per month.
4. When I phoned the _____ about our _____, he said it hadn't even been _____ from their depot.
5. The _____ department is responsible for checking all finished goods before they are packed.
6. _____ who can't _____ on time will not survive.

6 *Transfer*

PAIR WORK (Partner B turn to the Key section)

A: You are to telephone your supplier concerning the following order:

Order no:	XY/554/22
Product:	Electric irons
Quantity:	500
Delivery date:	21 March
Today's date:	15 April

UNIT 7
Promotion

The promotion mix consists of four major tools: advertising, sales promotion, public relations and personal selling.

Section A: Communication and advertising

Part 1: Choosing the message

1 *Warm-up*

Consider the following three products:

(i) A new brand of toothpaste
(ii) A new sports car
(iii) A new crop spray

Put yourself in the position of the potential consumer of each product. What sort of message would appeal to you?

2 *Reading*

Read the following extract. As you read it, summarise the content of this extract by completing Chart 7.1.

Having defined the target audience, the marketer must develop an effective message. Ideally, the message should attract *attention*, hold *interest*, arouse *desire* and elicit *action* (AIDA model).

Formulating the message will require solving four problems: what to say (message content), how to say it logically (message structure), how to say it symbolically (message format) and who should say it (message source).

Formulating the *message content* is a question of distinguishing between different kinds of appeal or USP (unique selling proposition). It consists of formulating some kind of benefit, motivation, identification, or reason why the audience should think about the product.

Rational appeals appeal to the audience's need for knowledge about the product. They respond to information about quality, economy, value and performance. *Emotional appeals* attempt to stir up some negative or positive emotion that will motivate purchase. The message can work with fear, guilt or shame to get people to do things (e.g. brush their teeth) or stop people from doing things (e.g. smoking, overeating). Positive emotions like humour, love, pride and joy can be induced to create a liking for a product.

Finally, *moral appeals* are directed at an audience's sense of right and wrong. They are often used to exhort people to support social causes such as a cleaner environment, equal rights for women, etc.

There are three aspects to message structure which should be considered. *Conclusion drawing* is the question of whether the message should draw a definite conclusion for the audience or leave it to them. Drawing an obvious conclusion may cause negative reactions if the audience resents the attempt to influence it, is annoyed at the attempt to explain the obvious or finds the issue highly personal.

One- or two-sided arguments raises the question whether the message should only praise the product or also mention some shortcomings. Research seems to show that two-sided arguments work best with audiences who are sceptical or well-informed. *Order of presentation* raises the question whether the strongest argument should be presented first or last.

We can look at message format from written, spoken and non-verbal points of view. In a print ad, the advertiser has to decide on the wording of the headline and the copy and on the layout and colour of the ad. On the radio, the advertiser must think about the wording, the voice quality and maybe music. If the message is to be carried on TV or in person, non-verbal clues such as facial expressions, gestures, dress and posture are also important.

Finally, messages delivered by attractive sources achieve higher attention and recall. Celebrities are likely to be most effective when they have credibility. Pharmaceutical companies want doctors to testify for their product's benefits because doctors have high credibility. Three factors seem to lie behind credibility: *expertise*, *trustworthiness* and *likeability*.

Chart 7.1   Factors influencing effectiveness of message

Message content (appeals)	Message structure (arguments)	Message format (visual/oral)	Message source (credibility)
a. _____	d. _____	g. _____	j. _____
b. _____	e. _____	h. _____	k. _____
c. _____	f. _____	i. _____	l. _____

3   Comprehension/interpretation

Decide on the message content, structure, format and source for the following three products:

(i) A toothpaste
(ii) A sports car
(iii) A crop spray (agricultural)

4   Language focus

4.1   Verb + preposition (see Unit 31 in *Language Reference for Business English*)

Look at the following sentences taken from the Reading passage:

'Rational appeals *appeal to* the audience's need for knowledge about the product.'
'We can *look at* message format from written, spoken and non-verbal points of view.'

Now complete the following sentences with the correct preposition:

1. We are looking _____ a message which really appeals _____ the audience. So far we haven't found one.
2. One strong emotional appeal nowadays is the environment. Looking _____ the environment well carries a strong appeal.
3. We can't decide _____ the message format. We need to look _____ a strong non-verbal approach.
4. People tend to look _____ to expert figures such as doctors.
5. We were thinking _____ doing the ad on television.
6. He insisted _____ using a balanced argument to present the product.
7. I was very annoyed _____ the simplicity of the arguments. Consumers like to think _____ the product.
8. If you look _____ the word in the dictionary, it means all communication which is non-verbal.
9. Have you heard _____ Professor Stell? He's very well known in his field.
10. We've looked _____ the question of hiring professional actors. It's much too expensive.

4.2   Verb + infinitive/verb + (preposition) + **ing** (see Unit 14 in *Language Reference for Business English*)

Look at the following sentences taken from the Reading passage:

'To get people *to do* things or stop people *from doing* things . . .'

Now complete the sentences with either an infinitive or (preposition) + **ing**

1. He accused me _____ my talent cheaply. (sell)
2. They liked _____ cowboy films. (watch)
3. He insisted _____ all the way through the film. (talk)
4. We were prevented _____ the building. (enter)
5. He hated _____ to the radio. (listen)
6. We are very keen _____ to classical music. (listen)
7. They loved _____ music together. (play)
8. They attempted _____ the film rights. (sell)
9. We were forced _____ on an unknown actress. (rely)
10. We were stopped _____ outside the hall. (demonstrate)

5   Word study

Match the characteristics/feelings on the right with the five headings on the left:

1. Rational	a. annoyed
	b. happy
	c. trustworthy
	d. well-dressed
2. Emotional – positive	e. sceptical
	f. resentful
	g. proud
	h. sincere
3. Emotional – negative	i. smart
	j. well-informed
	k. joyful
	l. credible
4. Credibility	m. guilty
	n. pretty
	o. knowledgeable
	p. angry
5. Appearance	q. attractive
	r. honest
	s. well-educated
	t. fearful

6 Transfer

Brief an advertising agency about the concept and message which you think is appropriate for the following product:

Product: dental chewing gum
Name: Dentigum
Benefits: prevents decay, tastes good
Features: low-price, regular use, conveniently packaged
Distribution: (i) pharmacies, (ii) general stores

Use Chart 7.1 to structure your presentation.

Part 2: Choosing the media

1 Warm-up

Which media would you choose for the following products and target audiences:

(i) Perfume → 25–35 year old women
(ii) A low-price automatic camera → men and women 20–40 years old
(iii) An expensive lawn-mower → 40–60 year old men

2 Listening

Listen to an extract from a meeting in which product and advertising managers are discussing the media mix for a new line in trainers aimed at teenagers. As you listen, complete Chart 7.2 by indicating with a tick (✓) which media is preferred.

Chart 7.2

	TV	Radio	Newspapers	Magazines	Outdoor
John Pete Mike Sheila					

3 Comprehension/interpretation

Grade the above media in terms of the following criteria (1 = best, 5 = worst):

1. Relative cost
2. Flexibility (booking, planning, lead time)
3. Reach (percentage of target audience exposed to advertisement)
4. Attention (percentage of target audience interested in the advertisement)
5. Selectivity (accuracy of media in reaching right audience)

4 Language focus

4.1 Suggest/recommend (see Unit 81 in *Language Reference for Business English*)

Look at the following sentences taken from the Listening passage:

> '*I'd recommend* we think in terms of twenty peak time slots . . .'
> '*Maybe we could consider* TV to establish a brand image . . .'

Now make suggestions/recommendations from the following prompts:

1. I / propose / invest / TV advertising
2. He / suggest / use / outside advertising
3. They / recommend / forget / radio
4. We / consider / place / print ads / prestige magazines
5. He / advise / us / reduce / advertising budget
6. I'd like / suggest / look at / new media
7. We / strongly recommend / you / study / TV ratings
8. Let us / think / targeted ads / trade journals

4.2 Emphasis – word order (see Unit 70 in *Language Reference for Business English*)

Look at the following sentences taken from the Listening passage:

> '*What I suggest we do is* go for ten slots . . .'

Now change the following sentences so that they are more emphatic:

1. We should target this age group very carefully.
   What we _____ .
2. We need to concentrate on direct sales.
3. They must reduce their advertising budget.
4. I recommend you try to reach the department stores.
5. We feel you have missed an opportunity.
6. They thought we had spent too much on outdoor advertising.
7. He expected us to hire a professional singer.
8. I propose you limit your advertising to radio.

5 Word study

Match the words/expressions in the left-hand column with their definitions/explanations in the right:

Words/expressions	Definitions/explanations
1. a slot	a. 7–9 p.m.
2. exposure	b. point-of-sale incentives to buy
3. peak/prime	c. up-market, expensive-looking
4. to sell in	d. an occasion when an ad is broadcast
5. to hit	e. customers who buy after the product has been adopted
6. word of mouth	f. to reach
7. sales promotion	g. amount of time the target audience sees/hears an ad
8. initiators	h. by personal recommendation
9. followers	i. customers who buy first/are prepared to experiment
10. glossy	j. to promote products to middlemen (wholesalers and retailers)

6 Transfer

Discuss the media mix which you feel would be appropriate for:

Product:	a new line in fashionable sports clothing
Producer:	well-known name in sports sector
Price:	high price
Target:	men and women 30–45 years old
Objective:	to achieve market share first, profits second

Section B: Personal selling

Part 1: Selling styles

1 Warm-up

1.1 How do you react to the 'hard sell'?
1.2 What characteristics should a good salesperson have?

2 *Reading*

Read the extract about selling styles. As you read it, plot the five selling styles mentioned in Chart 7.3.

Selling styles differ in many ways but one fundamental difference is between the sales-oriented and the customer-oriented approach. The first one concentrates on high-pressure techniques such as those used in selling encyclopaedias and cars. The techniques include overstating the product's merits, criticizing competitive products, using a slick pre-prepared sales presentation, selling yourself and offering some concession to get the order on the spot. This form of selling assumes that the customers are not likely to buy except under pressure, that they will be influenced by a slick presentation and ingratiating manners, and that they will not be sorry after signing the order, or if they are, it doesn't matter.

In the customer-oriented approach, the salesperson learns how to listen and question in order to identify customer needs and come up with good product solutions. Presentation skills are secondary to needs analysis skills. This approach assumes that customers have latent needs that constitute company opportunities, that they appreciate good suggestions and that they will be loyal to representatives who have their long-term interests at heart. The problem-solver is a more compatible image for the salesperson under the marketing concept than the hard-seller or order-taker.

Blake and Mouton distinguish various selling styles by examining these two dimensions: concern for the sale and concern for the customer (see Chart 7.3).

Type 1 is very much the order-taker. He places the product before the customer and expects it to sell itself. If it doesn't, it doesn't matter. Type 2 is similar in that he also shows little concern for the customer but differs in that he is very concerned to get the sale; he pushes the product, piling on the pressure to ensure he gets the sale.

Type 3 falls somewhere in the middle of the chart. He has a tried and tested technique blending customer concern with product emphasis; this is what is often called the soft sell.

Type 4 is very customer-oriented; the other extreme to the type 2 hard-seller. He aims to be the customer's friend, to understand him, develop a bond which ties him to the salesman and therefore the product.

Finally, type 5 is similar to type 4 in that he also shows concern for the customer but in a more impersonal way. He aims to consult with the customer, acquaint himself with the needs and then work towards a sound purchase decision. This problem-solving mentality is more compatible with the total marketing concept.

Blake and Mouton argue that no one sales style will be effective with all buyers. Buying styles are just as varied as selling styles. Buyers vary in their concern for the purchase and concern for the salesperson. Some buyers couldn't care less; some are defensive, some will only listen to salespersons from well-known companies.

Chart 7.3

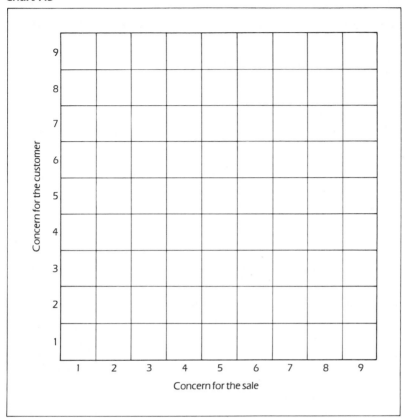

3 Comprehension/interpretation

Which of the above selling styles (type 1–5) do you feel would work best with the following buyers:

1. Print buyer for a large advertising department. Wants a working relationship with the seller but has no time or inclination to get to know his supplier well. Needs a relatively simple presentation of what the seller has to offer in order to meet his needs.
2. Regional purchasing manager of textile company. Believes relationship with the supplier is the most important thing. Will only deal with salespeople she gets on with and can build a long-term relationship with.
3. Department store buyer of clothes. Sees a lot of salespeople. She is interested in knowing the seller's product and its price and that's all. She has no time for any extras.
4. Training manager of a large multinational company. She is looking for a supplier to act as a consultant and provider of training for a new ambitious sales training programme.

4 Language focus

4.1 Similarity and difference (see Unit 72 in *Language Reference for Business English*)

Look at the following sentences taken from the Reading passage:

'Selling styles *differ in* many ways but one fundamental *difference is between* . . .'
'Type 2 is *similar in* that he also shows concern for the customer . . .'

Complete the following sentences with an appropriate word/phrase expressing similarity or difference:

1. Selling techniques _____ depending on the type of customer and product.
2. There is a big _____ selling a car and selling a consultancy service.
3. All customers are _____ in one sense. They are all interested in value for money.
4. Selling styles _____ one country _____ another. A door-to-door salesman in Japan behaves _____ one in the US.
5. We can _____ two distinct styles: the product-oriented and the customer-oriented.
6. There are many _____ in selling services. Concern for the customer is _____ to all services.

4.2 Reflexive pronouns (see Unit 56 in *Language Reference for Business English*)

Look at the following sentences taken from the Reading passage:

'The techniques include selling *yourself* . . .'
'He places the product before the customer and expects it to sell *itself*.'

Now decide whether you need a reflexive pronoun or not in the following sentences. If so, insert the correct form.

1. We congratulated _____. Nobody else said anything.
2. The problem with selling _____ is that there's nobody else who can replace you.
3. We were invited _____ to a sales conference in Harrogate.
4. Where's your invitation? – I haven't got one. I invited _____ .
5. New products rarely sell _____. You have to inform the market _____ .
6. One shouldn't only think of _____. There are others to consider.
7. I _____ would like to go home. My wife _____ wants to stay.
8. Cars, in _____, should be commodities. However, marketing has transformed them into consumer goods.

5 Word study

Match the words/expressions on the left with their opposites on the right:

1. sales-oriented	a. impersonal
2. hard sell	b. compatible
3. high pressure	c. open
4. tried and tested	d. latent
5. personal	e. customer-oriented
6. defensive	f. loyal
7. closed	g. direct
8. overstatement	h. support
9. criticism	i. soft sell
10. pre-prepared	j. approachable
11. ingratiating	k. relaxed
12. surface	l. experimental
13. fickle	m. understatement
14. poorly matched	n. spontaneous

6 Transfer

The company you have been called in to consult (Buromat, Inc., an office supplies company) has used a very carefully designed sales style for many years (see type 3 above). This has worked well for a long time, but in an increasingly complex and competitive market, it seems to lack flexibility. Their typical buyers are small to medium-sized companies where the purchaser is either the office manager or an administration manager. These buyers are demanding but lack time to give to salespeople. Use Chart 7.3 to present alternative approaches and then recommend the sort of selling style you feel is appropriate to this company.

Part 2: Selling tactics

1 Warm-up

1.1 How important is it for a salesperson to ask questions?
1.2 What sorts of question should a salesperson ask?

2 Listening

Listen to the sales call. As you listen, complete the checklist in Chart 7.4.

Chart 7.4

SALES CALL CHECKLIST

Prospect: Davidson & Sons
Size   20 employees
Business: Management Consultants

Situation:

Type of correspondence   a. _____
Amount of correspondence   b. _____
Person responsible   c. _____

d. **Problem:** (tick or cross)
 (i)   No clear responsibility
 (ii) Post Office too far
 (iii) Takes too long

Need:

e. _____

Any objections:

f. _____

Solution:

g. _____

Additional benefits:

h. _____

---

3 Comprehension/interpretation

3.1 How would you describe the salesperson's approach?

- hard sell/soft sell
- sales-oriented/customer-oriented
- talking/listening
- leading/non-directed

3.2 Do you think he was a good salesperson? Would you recommend any improvements?

4 Language focus

4.1   Question techniques (see Unit 38 in *Language Reference for Business English*)

Look at the following sentences taken from the Listening passage:

> '*Could you tell me what sort of correspondence goes out from this company?*'
> '*That could be more when you're doing a mailshot . . . ?*'

Look at the following three types of question:

Indirect (polite):	Could you tell me what . . . ?
Direct:	What . . . / Do you . . . ?
Leading:	That could be more (couldn't it)?

Change the following questions as indicated:

1. Could you tell me why you don't have a computer?
   Direct: _____
2. How many employees do you have?
   Indirect: _____
3. Do you plan to take on more employees?
   Leading: _____
4. Are you finding business more difficult at the moment?
   Leading: _____
5. Would you mind telling me if you have any problems recruiting staff?
   Direct: _____
6. Do you pay over the market rate?
   Indirect: _____
7. Have you fired anybody recently?
   Indirect: _____
8. Could you tell me whether you are a director?
   Leading: _____
9. You're facing severe financial difficulties, aren't you?
   Direct: _____
10. You don't intend to stay in business any longer, do you?
    Indirect: _____

5 Word study

Time is sometimes an obsession, sometimes an excuse, and often a luxury. Below are some expressions associated with time. Group the expressions on the right under the headings on the left:

Headings	Expressions
1. Lack of time	a. How long does it take?
	b. I'm short of time
	c. I've got plenty of time
2. Surplus of time	d. I'll have to cut short the meeting
	e. Time is money
	f. I'm in a hurry
3. Length of time	g. We'll have to prolong the project
	h. A couple of hours
	i. It takes a good twenty minutes
4. Reducing time	j. It'll last longer than we thought
	k. Time never stands still
	l. I'm rushed off my feet
5. Extending time	m. I've got time to spare
	n. We'll have to have a guillotine on this
6. Time idioms	o. Time is of the essence
	p. Never in a month of Sundays
	q. Once in a blue moon
7. Infrequency	r. Time is pressing
	s. Every once in a while
	t. Now and then
	u. Off and on

6 Transfer

PAIR WORK (Partner B turn to the Key section)

A: You want to sell an automatic office coffee machine to your partner B. S/he is the office manager for a firm of lawyers. You have managed to make an appointment but you know s/he will be short of time. Use the checklist (Chart 7.5) to conduct the sales call.

Chart 7.5

SALES CALL CHECKLIST

Situation:
No. of employees: _____
No. of visitors: _____
Present coffee-making facilities: _____

Problem:
Time to get a coffee?
Quality of coffee?
Quantity of coffee?
Cost of coffee?

Need:

Objections:

Solution:

Three models:	The Coffeemaker (makes enough for 6 cups)	cost: £45.00
	The Coffeemaker Plus (12 cups)	cost: £60.00
	The Coffeemaker Deluxe (12 cups + alarm when ready)	cost: £75.00

UNIT 8
International marketing

Breaking into foreign markets presents special difficulties. Although the same marketing concepts and strategies apply, cultural, political and economic differences make the task of entering an overseas market more risky.

Section A: Entering foreign markets

Part 1: Ways of entering a foreign market

1 Warm-up

1.1 What problems does a company face in trying to enter a foreign market?
1.2 What is the simplest way for a company to enter a foreign market?

2 Reading

Read the extract about entering foreign markets. As you read it, complete Chart 8.1.

The simplest way to enter a foreign market is through exporting. The company may passively export its surpluses, or it may make a commitment to expand exports to a particular market. In either case the company produces all its goods in the home country though it may make changes to them for the export market. There are two types of exporting: indirect and direct. Indirect exporting means working through independent middlemen such as agents and dealers. Indirect exporting can be done with little investment and therefore involves less risk. Mistakes can be made but they shouldn't be too costly.

Direct exporting involves setting up an export department or even an overseas sales branch which actively uses the company's own employees. This will give the seller more presence and control in the market but obviously means heavier investment.

A second method of entering a foreign market is through joint ventures with foreign companies. There are four types of joint venture.

Licensing is the simplest way for a manufacturer to produce its goods in the foreign market. The company enters into an agreement with a licensee offering the right to use a manufacturing process, trademark, patent or other item of value for a fee or royalty. Once again the company gains entry into the market at little risk but there are potential disadvantages. The company has less control over the licensee than if it had set up its own production facilities. If the licensee is very successful, the company has given up the potential for large profits and, if and when the contract ends, it may find it has created a competitor.

Another option is *contract manufacturing*. This means contracting with foreign manufacturers to produce the product. It has the drawback of less control over the manufacturing process and the loss of potential profits on manufacturing. On the other hand, it offers the company the chance to get off to a quicker start and take on less risk. There is also the opportunity to form a partnership or buy out the local manufacturer later.

Joint ownership ventures consist of the company joining with foreign investors to create a local business in which they share joint ownership and control. Joint ownership may make sense for political or economic reasons. Sometimes foreign governments make joint ownership a condition for entry. It also has certain drawbacks. Above all, there is the danger of disagreement over crucial issues such as investment and marketing. One firm may want to put money back into the company while the other wants to take it out.

Besides exporting and joint ventures, there is also the possibility of direct investment – in other words developing foreign-based assembly or manufacturing facilities. If the foreign market is large enough, local production facilities offer many advantages. The company may have lower costs in the form of cheaper labor, raw materials and transport/distribution. The company will gain a better image in the host country because it creates jobs. It also develops a deeper relationship with government, customers, suppliers and distributors. Finally, by direct investment, the company keeps full control over investment and marketing policies. The main disadvantage is that the firm faces many risks such as devalued currencies, declining markets or even government takeover.

Chart 8.1

Method of entry		Advantages	Disadvantages
1. Export	1.1 Indirect		
	1.2 Direct		
2. Joint venture	2.1 Licensing		
	2.2 Contract manufacturing		
	2.3 Joint ownership		
3. Direct investment			

3 Comprehension/interpretation

3.1 Why do you think joint ventures, rather than direct investment, are becoming more common in international trade?

3.2 Setting up a foreign subsidiary is a large investment for the parent company. Do you think the senior management positions should be held by local or headquarters staff?

4 Language focus

4.1 **Make** and **do** (see Unit 30 in *Language Reference for Business English*)

Look at the following sentences taken from the Reading passage:

'It may *make* a commitment to expand exports . . .'
'Indirect exporting can be *done* with little investment . . .'

Now complete the following sentences with an appropriate form of **make** or **do**:

1. We _____ the mistake of setting up a joint venture.
2. There's a lot of work to _____ before setting up in a foreign country.
3. He _____ the job of importing goods from the Far East.
4. The government _____ us register the company locally.
5. If we had _____ our homework, we wouldn't have _____ the investment.
6. It's important to _____ friends in high places.
7. Deals like that are _____ on the ground. You can't _____ business with these people without meeting them.
8. We could _____ without interference from politicians but we _____ the best of the situation.
9. He _____ very well to establish the business. It's a pity he didn't _____ more money.
10. In order to _____ this work, we're going to have to _____ a lot of research.

4.2   Verb + preposition (see Unit 31 in *Language Reference for Business English*)

Look at the following sentences taken from the Reading passage:

'Direct exporting involves *setting up* an export department . . .'
'It offers the company the chance to *get off* to a quicker start . . .'

Now complete the following sentences with the correct preposition:

1. They put a lot of money _____ the project.
2. The project had to be put _____ due to production delays.
3. Once we had got _____ the joint venture, it was very difficult to get _____ of it.
4. Companies are often unwilling to give _____ their independence.
5. I'd like to take _____ your offer of collaboration.
6. The company was put _____ by the size of the investment. They decided instead to go _____ partnership with a local firm.
7. They made _____ for their lack of financial investment by doing a lot of the ground work.
8. We could only pull _____ of the joint venture if they gave _____ their position in the market.

5   Word study

Complete the following table:

Country	Inhabitant	Language
United States	American	English
France		
China		
Japan		
Brazil		
Spain		
Sweden		
United Kingdom		
Germany		
Netherlands		

6   Transfer

Your company manufactures electrical measurement equipment. You have a well developed local market in which your products are well known to industrial companies. However, you have not yet broken into any foreign markets. Use Chart 8.1 to discuss the options open to your company. Use your specialised knowledge of your home and foreign markets.

Part 2: Learning from mistakes in foreign markets

1 Warm-up

1.1 How quickly should a company expect to see a return on its investment when entering a foreign market?

1.2 How important do you think it is to employ local staff when entering a foreign market?

2 Listening

Listen to the meeting where the failure to penetrate export markets is being discussed. As you listen, complete Chart 8.2.

Chart 8.2

Country	Strategy	Mistake	Recommendation
France			
Germany			
Sweden			

3 Comprehension/interpretation

If you were recruiting a sales representative to help you penetrate a foreign market, how would you rank the following skills-characteristics:

a. Knowledge of the local market
b. Knowledge of the product sector
c. Selling skills
d. Knowledge of local language
e. International experience

4 Language focus

4.1 Conditional III (see Unit 10 in *Language Reference for Business English*)

Look at the following sentences taken from the Listening passage:

'Our results *would have been* better *if we'd relied* less on agents . . .'
'*If I'd known* how conservative German customers were going to be, I *would have recommended* a joint venture . . .'

Now complete the following sentences by putting the verbs in the right form.

---

1. If we _____ (do) research beforehand, we _____ (not make) so many mistakes.
2. We _____ (never enter) the market if we _____ (know) the problems.
3. In hindsight, we _____ (do) better, if we _____ (concentrate) on big firms.
4. Looking back on it, we _____ (penetrate) the market if we _____ (not use) agents.
5. If only I _____ (know), I _____ never (recommend) it.
6. We _____ not (be) where we are today, if we _____ (not take) risks.

4.2 Chairing (see Skill 2 in *Language Reference for Business English*)

Look at the following extracts from the Listening passage:

'Geoff, why don't you start with France?'
'So what you're saying is . . .'

Match the expressions with their chairing function:

Chairing functions
1. Opening the meeting
2. Agreeing objectives
3. Inviting someone to start
4. Paraphrasing/clarifying
5. Shutting someone up
6. Encouraging others
7. Keeping the meeting going
8. Dealing with digressions
9. Summarising
10. Closing the meeting

Expressions
a. So what you're saying is
b. We haven't heard from everybody
c. Let's get down to business
d. Let me just recap then
e. That's interesting Michael, let's hear from the rest
f. We are here today to discuss the following three points
g. I think we're getting off the point. Let's get back to . . .
h. Let's call it a day
i. Peter, would you like to start?
j. Time is short, I suggest we move on

5 Word study

Complete the phrase by matching the word/expression on the left with its best association on the right:

1. to break into
2. to learn from
3. to look
4. to rely less
5. to have a
6. conservative
7. to establish
8. someone
9. it counts
10. a much reduced

a. on the ground
b. your mistakes
c. a feel for
d. a market
e. budget
f. a presence
g. in detail
h. customers
i. on agents
j. for a lot

Section B: Global versus local marketing

Part 1: The world's champion marketers: the Japanese?

1 Warm-up

Why do you think the Japanese have been so successful in penetrating international markets?

2 Reading

Read the following extract about the Japanese. After you have read it, complete the true/false exercise which follows.

Few dispute that the Japanese have performed an economic miracle since World War II. In a very short time, they have achieved global market leadership in many industries: cars, motorcycles, watches, cameras, optical instruments, steel, shipbuilding, computers and consumer electronics. They are now making strong inroads into rubber tyres, chemicals, machine tools and even designer clothes and cosmetics. Some credit the global success of Japanese companies to their unique business and management practices. Others point to the help they get from Japanese government, powerful trading companies, and banks. Still others say Japan's success is based on low wage rates and unfair dumping policies.

But one of the main keys to Japan's success is its skilful use of marketing. They know how to select a market, enter it the right way, build market share, and protect their share against competitors.

Selecting markets

The Japanese work hard to identify attractive global markets. They look for industries that require high skills and high labor intensity but few natural resources. These include consumer electronics, cameras and pharmaceuticals. They like markets where consumers around the world would be willing to buy the same product design. They look for industries where the market leaders are weak or complacent.

Entering markets

Japanese study teams spend several months evaluating the target market, searching for market niches that are not being satisfied. Sometimes they start with a low-price, stripped-down version of a product, sometimes with a product that is as good as the competition's but priced lower, sometimes with a product with higher quality or new features. The Japanese line up good distribution in order to provide quick service to their customers. They use advertising to bring their products to the customer's attention. Their entry strategy is to build market share rather than early profits. The Japanese often are willing to wait even a decade before realising their profits.

Building market share

Once Japanese firms gain a market foothold, they begin to expand their market share. They pour money into product improvements and new models so that they can offer more and better things than the competition. They spot new opportunities through market segmentation, develop markets in new countries, and work to build a network of world markets and production locations.

Protecting market share

Once the Japanese achieve market leadership, they become defenders rather than attackers. Their defense strategy is to continue product development and refine market segmentation.

Now indicate whether the following statements are true (T) or false (F).

1. Most people don't agree that the Japanese have performed an economic miracle.
2. Most people agree that the main reason for Japan's success is their unique management practices.
3. The Japanese select industries where they don't need large workforces.
4. They select industries where the competition is asleep.
5. They always enter the market by undercutting the competition's prices.
6. They look for a fairly quick return on investment.
7. They concentrate on market growth rather than profitability.
8. Throughout the product life cycle they aggressively market against the competition.

3 Comprehension/interpretation

Look at the above eight statements and judge whether your company/country shares the same views/strategies.

4 Language focus

4.1 Determiners: **a/an, the**, ∅ (see Unit 55 in *Language Reference for Business English*)

Look at the following sentence taken from the Reading passage:

'Few dispute that *the* Japanese have performed *an* economic miracle since ∅ World War II.'

Now complete the following passage by inserting: **a/an, the** or ∅ (nothing).

_____ economy is moving into _____ recession. This is characterised by _____ high inflation, _____ rising unemployment and _____ very low growth rate. What is particularly worrying is _____ large number of bankruptcies that have been reported. It seems that _____ firms are going into _____ liquidation at _____ alarming rate. _____ major reason for this is

_____ high interest rates. During _____ eighties, firms grew rapidly, and in order to finance _____ growth they borrowed _____ lot of money from _____ banks. Now in _____ time of contraction, they are unable to repay _____ loans.

4.2 Determiners: **much/many, little/few** (see Units 58 and 59 in _Language Reference for Business English_)

Look at the following sentence taken from the Reading passage:

'They look for industries which require high skills and high labor intensity but _few_ natural resources.'

Now complete the following sentences with:

much   many   few (fewer)   little (less)

1. There are _____ natural resources in Japan than most developed countries.
2. _____ Japanese firms are looking for quick profits.
3. There isn't _____ information about internal strategy.
4. There's too _____ information about Japanese long-term plans.
5. _____ higher investment is needed by European companies if they want to compete against the Japanese.
6. There is _____ long-term planning in the US than in Japan.
7. There are many _____ US companies established in Japan than vice versa.
8. In my opinion, there is too _____ talk and too _____ action.

5 Word study

Match the words/expressions on the left (all taken from the extract) with the most appropriate equivalent on the right:

1. to make inroads into		a.	unprotected
2. to credit		b.	basic
3. dumping		c.	to make liquid
4. skills		d.	to improve
5. weak		e.	to penetrate
6. complacent		f.	to establish a share
7. niches		g.	to identify
8. stripped-down		h.	to believe
9. to line up		i.	loss-making exporting
10. to realise		j.	to develop
11. to gain a foothold		k.	to invest heavily
12. to pour money into		l.	abilities
13. to spot		m.	defined market segment
14. to refine		n.	sleepy

6 Transfer

Discuss with your partners the differences between the Japanese approach to global marketing and that of your own country.

Part 2: Corporate versus subsidiary strategy

1 Warm-up

1.1 In a local market (one country) what advantages does a multinational company have over a national company?

1.2 What do most consumers think of multinational companies?

2 Listening

Listen to the extract from a meeting between a representative from corporate headquarters in America and the marketing manager of a recently acquired Japanese company. As you listen complete Chart 8.3.

Chart 8.3

Corporate strategy: Objective 1: _____ Objective 2: _____ **Local objections to:** Objective 1: _____ Objective 2: _____

3 Comprehension/interpretation

3.1 Do you think Mr Stone handles this meeting well?

3.2 Do you think Mr Tokaido handles this meeting well?

3.3 If you were in their shoes, would you approach the problem differently?

4 Language focus

4.1 Participating in meetings (see Skill 2 in *Language Reference for Business English*)

Look at the following sentence taken from the Listening passage:

'I appreciate your concern but I think you have to see . . .'

Now match the expressions below with the appropriate function:

Functions	*Expressions*
1. Summarising/paraphrasing	a. I can't see how we can use
	b. I'm sure you'd agree
2. Showing understanding	c. To put it another way
	d. I really don't think it will help
3. Introducing concerns	e. Sorry to interrupt you
	f. What worries us here is
4. Interrupting	g. I appreciate your concern
	h. I think you have to see
5. Persuading	i. I'm sorry to put this so bluntly
	j. There, if you don't mind me saying,
6. Disagreeing	you're wrong!
	k. To summarise

5 Word study

Find the opposites of the following words and expressions. Use a dictionary if necessary.

1. high profile
2. to stand alone
3. long-established
4. presence
5. excellent results
6. to be aware
7. well-segmented
8. strongly linked
9. to diversify
10. to expand
11. to benefit from

6 Transfer

Present or discuss the benefits of a strong corporate identity from a global marketing point of view.

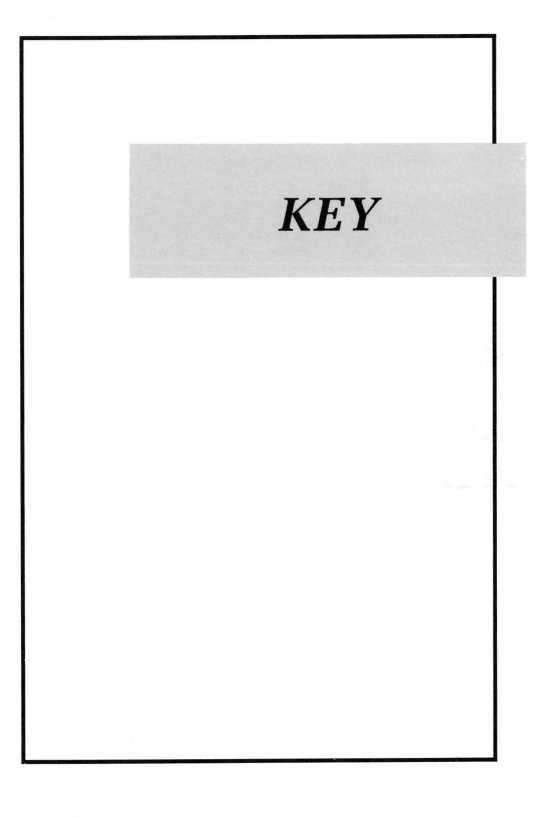

KEY

UNIT 1
The role of marketing

Section A: What is marketing?

Part 1: Some definitions of marketing

3 Comprehension/interpretation

3.1   1 and 2

3.2   4

3.3   7

3.4   5 and 8

4 Language focus

4.1   Adjectives

1. Our product is so successful that we are rapidly running out of stock.
2. Normally, we invest heavily at this time of year.
3. Profits have only slightly increased and therefore we have had to cut back on further investment.
4. Lately, he has been arriving late at every meeting.
5. The sales department performed well last year so we have given all the sales-people a generous bonus.
6. He worked so hard that he fell ill.

4.2   Adjective modification

1. She's very well qualified. I think she should get the job.
2. The computer program is tremendously complex. I can't understand it.
3. Normally the work is easy. This time it has proved unusually difficult.
4. He's technically oriented but not sufficiently commercial, so he'd make a good engineer but not a salesman.
5. The policy is not radically different from last year. Basically we will try to increase market share.

5 Word study

Verb	Noun
to decide	a decision
to sell	sales
to promote	promotion
to create	creation
to exchange	an exchange
to perform	performance
to act	an act/action
to produce	a producer
to consume	consumption
to communicate	communication
to deliver	a delivery

Part 2: Some conflicting management philosophies

Listening tapescript

1   As I see the problem, the major focus of investment must be in improving productivity. We've also got to make sure there are no delays in deliveries. In this way we can aim to bring down the price and make our products more readily available. We're in a mass market, where price and availability are what matter most to our customers.

2   I think we'd all agree with you as far as you go. But I feel what we are still failing to do is to establish a strong enough brand. The only way we can do this in an increasingly competitive market is to increase our budgets in advertising and make our salesforce even more effective.

3   I'm not sure I agree with either of you. You are both taking a too restricted view, looking at it from the inside-out. What we need is to take an outside-in approach. What I mean by this is we've got to get to know our customers better, what their needs and wants are. If we are just production- or sales-oriented, that'll keep the turnover going in the short term but we've got to stay ahead of the competition in the long term. No, I feel we must certainly ensure quality and price for our existing products and of course promote them well, but above all we need to look to the future – a strategy for the next twenty years in terms of growth. This means better market research – generally a more integrated approach.

4   Geoff takes the longer-term view but I feel he misses an important dimension. It's not enough to focus just on our customers' present and future needs. We have to take a wider view – there are strong pressures in society now which have little to do with individual needs and wants – I'm thinking of the environment in particular. I feel we need to look at what type of world we are . . .

5   Oh, come on Julie. Let's get back down to earth. This company has made its name and its money by being first in the field in new areas. You only have to look at the Japanese to see what they're spending on R&D. Product innovation is where the future is . . .

2   Listening

Speakers	Concept
1	A
2	C
3	D
4	E
5	B

3   Comprehension/interpretation

3.1   Improve productivity.
3.2   Outside-in approach, improve market research.
3.3   Society (in particular environment).
3.4   Successful research and development.

4 Language focus

4.1 Opinion-giving

1. In my opinion
2. What we must do is
3. I feel
4. I tend to think

5. I'm sure that
6. We could discuss
7. It's certain
8. From this point of view

4.2 Agreeing and disagreeing

1. e   2. d   3. f   4. a   5. b   6. c

5 Word study

1. improvement — deterioration
2. available — unavailable
3. competitive — uncompetitive
4. effective — ineffective
5. inside-out — outside-in
6. investment — disinvestment/divestiture
7. to bring down prices — to increase/put up prices
8. to stay ahead — to fall behind
9. mass-market — niche market

Section B: Marketing planning

Part 1: Strategic planning

2 Reading

In Chart 1.1:

a. Detailed supporting objectives
b. Decide portfolio of business
c. Develop marketing plan

In Chart 1.2:

a. To fight world hunger
b. To research into new fertilizers
c. To improve profits
d. To increase sales
e. Increase share of US market
f. To enter foreign markets
g. Increase product's availability and promotion
h. Cut prices and call on large farms

3 Comprehension/interpretation

3.1 According to Levitt, it would be better to state it in terms of customer needs.
3.2 This is too broad. It sounds pretentious.
3.3 To provide funds for research.

4 Language focus

4.1 Sequence

1. c   2. e   3. h   4. g   5. a   6. d   7. b   8. f

4.2 Expressing purpose

1. c   2. b   3. d   4. e   5. a

5 Word study

1. d   2. f   3. k   4. i   5. a   6. j   7. e   8. b   9. h   10. g   11. c

Part 2: Portfolio analysis

Listening tapescript

I'd like to analyse our current position in terms of market growth and market share. This will help us to formulate strategies to meet our customers' needs in the next ten years. So, I'm going to divide my presentation into three parts. Firstly an analysis of our main business areas, secondly our objectives for these business areas, and finally strategies to achieve these objectives.

Right, to start with the analysis. If you look at this chart, you'll see market growth rate on the vertical axis – this is an index of market attractiveness. And then on the horizontal axis relative market share broadly broken down into high and low.

Now, as you can see the chart is divided into four quadrants. Let's start with the bottom left quadrant. Here we have our cash cow, as we have had for many years, the XT2500. We still have nearly 25 per cent market share of the mainframe market and, as a result, nearly 50 per cent of our profits are generated by sales of this product.

So, let's move on to the next quadrant – here in the bottom right, we are in the process of phasing out the XT380, our mini system. Clearly we cannot expect any further growth in this area, given the declining growth and share rates.

Right, let's move on up to the top half of the matrix. Here in the top right quadrant we've got our new XT25B – the micro targeted at the educational market. Basically, as you know, despite initial successes, we have failed to build up any significant share of this market. However, on the other hand, we mustn't forget that this is one of the fastest growing sectors of the market. That's why we can rightly call this a question mark product.

Finally and fortunately we still have our star, here in the top left-hand quadrant – the XT25, launched three years ago and still performing very well in the small business user market.

Right, that brings me to the second part of my presentation. What I'd like to do now is to present the objectives for these four products. Firstly, the XT2500 – our aim here should be to hold market share for at least the next five years. The fate of the XT380 has already been decided – we aim to phase it out in the next two years. Much more important is what we plan to do about the other two products. I feel strongly that we must aim to build on the very small market share presently held by the XT25B. As I've already pointed out, this is the fastest-growing market and we must increase our presence in it. Finally our star, I think we should be looking to further increase the share of the XT25 and I'll come to how I think we can achieve this in a minute. Right, are there any questions before I go on to the more detailed strategies to achieve these objectives.

2 Listening

In Chart 1.3:

a. star	d. market growth rate	g. XT380
b. XT25	e. low	h. high
c. XT25B	f. cash cow	i. market share

3 Comprehension/interpretation

3.1　(ii)　Objectives for business areas.
　　　(iii)　Strategies to achieve objectives.
3.2　Because they can be 'milked' for profits.
3.3　Because their future is uncertain.
3.4　Because they are the 'brightest' products the company has.
3.5　(i)　Hold market share for five years.
　　　(ii)　Phase out in next two years.
　　　(iii)　Build up market share.
　　　(iv)　Further increase market share.

4 Language focus

4.1　Introductions to presentations

1. b　　2. f　　3. h　　4. c　　5. e　　6. g　　7. i　　8. d　　9. a

4.2　Link phrases for presentations

1. c　　2. e　　3. i　　4. b　　5. f　　6. j　　7. a　　8. h　　9. d　　10. g

5 Word study

1.　a, d　　4.　e　　　7.　a, b
2.　d　　　5.　f　　　8.　a, c
3.　e　　　6.　a, b, d, f

UNIT 2
Analysis of market opportunities

Section A: Market research

Part 1: An overview of the market research process

2 *Reading*

In Chart 2.1:

a. Developing the research plan
b. Implementing the plan
c. Interpreting and presenting the findings

In Chart 2.2

a. Exploratory
b. Descriptive
c. Causal

d. Observational
e. Surveys
f. Experimental

g. Mail
h. Telephone
i. Personal interview

j. Sample unit
k. Sample size
l. Sampling procedure

m. Questionnaire
n. Mechanical instruments

3 *Comprehension/interpretation*

3.1   They didn't research the specific causes.
3.2   Would a discount sales promotion campaign achieve higher sales?
3.3   From various data banks.
3.4   Structure: controlled, measurable but not deep. Unstructured: deeper, spontaneous but open to bias and difficult to measure.
3.5   Possible steps:

1.   Set up two sample groups (target and control).
2.   Target group suffer from depression and are monitored during three month period.
3.   Control group do not suffer from depression and are monitored during three month period.
4.   Results of two groups analysed and compared with weather reports over the same period.

4 *Language focus*

4.1 Questions

1. Q: Could you tell me your name?
2. Q: And your surname?
3. Q: Do you live in this house here?
4. Q: How many of you live here?
5. Q: Do you work?
6. Q: What does your husband do?
7. Q: Who does he work for?

8. Q: Do you have a car?
9. Q: Which one do you drive?
10. Q: How old are your children?
11. Q: Where do you go for your holidays?
12. Q: When and how long do you go for?
13. Q: Do you fly?
14. Q: Are you going this year?

4.2 Modals

1. Entrance is forbidden. You must/may not enter.
2. Success is possible. We could/may be successful.
3. Participation is compulsory. We have to take part.
4. Permission is given. You may take the afternoon off.
5. Success is probable. We should succeed.

6. He has the ability. He can win the competition.
7. Participation is voluntary. We don't have to go to the reception.
8. Failure is impossible. We can't fail.
9. It's possible to segment the market. It can be segmented.
10. Permission is not given. You may not leave the building.

5 *Word study*

to explore	exploration	explorer	explorative
to respond	response	respondent	responsive
to describe	description	(describer)	descriptive
to analyse	analysis	analyst	analytical
to manage	management	manager	managerial
to hypothesise	hypothesis	(hypothesiser)	hypothetical
to observe	observation	observer	observational
to interpret	interpretation	interpreter	interpretative

(. . .) = not commonly used

Part 2: Contact methods used in market research

Listening tapescript

A: Right, we're here today to decide about which contact method to use for research into our new adventure holiday. We all know the choice available – we can go for mail, telephone or personal interviewing. John, I believe you are in favour of using mail?

B: That's right. We can make our sample large enough to give us truly representative results. In addition, the cost per respondent will be considerably lower than the other methods. But there's another factor – in my experience you tend to get more honest answers and this is because no interviewer is involved to influence the respondents.

C: All that's true but it's not the whole picture. Mail questionnaires are much less flexible – in other words there's no chance of adapting them to the particular respondent. They're also tremendously slow to implement and the response rate, as we all know, is much lower than with other methods. There's another point – in our case we're targeting adult males between 25 and 40 – we're going to have very little control over who answers the questions – in half the cases it'll probably be his wife or kids!

A: Okay, Susan, you've made your point. So what do you favour?

C: I reckon we should go for telephone interviewing. We're short of time and telephoning is the quickest method. It's also a lot more flexible than mail – the interviewers can adapt their questions to the particular respondent. There're another couple of advantages with telephoning – we've got much greater sample control – we can really make sure we're talking to the target males and our response rate will be much better.

B: True, Susan, but what about cost? That's going to be quite a lot higher. It's also less impartial. As I've already mentioned, you're bound to get quite a lot of interviewer bias.

A: Yes, I can see that. Michelle, we haven't heard from you.

D: Well, I'd go for personal interviewing. Not the usual individual street interviews but I reckon we should set up focus group interviews. This way we can invite carefully selected samples of our target group and really find out what they feel. We'll get a lot more information and insight and there's much more flexibility in terms of exploring our target's feelings and attitudes about the product. It won't take us long to set up and we know we'll get a good response rate.

B: But Michelle, that's going to push up our costs enormously. It also means we have to keep our sample size very small. Another thing – you say we get a lot more information, but how accurate will it be? The interviewer can introduce all sorts of bias which makes it very difficult for us to interpret the results.

A: Okay, I can see you've all come very well prepared. That's good, but now we're going to have to make a decision. Have you got the precise costings . . . ?

2   Listening

Chart 2.3

		Mail	Telephone	Personal
1.	Flexibility	✗	✓	✓✓
2.	Amount of data	✓✓	O	✓
3.	Control of bias	✓	✗	✗
4.	Control of sample	✗	✓	✓✓
5.	Speed of data collection	✗	✓✓	✓
6.	Response rate	✗	✓	✓✓
7.	Cost	✓✓	✗	✗

3   Comprehension/interpretation

3.1   The interviewer's personality affecting responses.

3.2   Target group receive too much 'junk' mail.

3.3   The main difference is that the participants in a focus group are specially chosen.

4 *Language focus*

4.1 Comparison of adjectives

1. more modern
2. easier
3. more interesting
4. better
5. worse

6. more direct
7. narrower
8. more superficial
9. funnier
10. higher

4.2 Adjective modification – degree

1. B   2. C   3. C   4. A   5. B   6. A   7. A   8. B   9. C

5 *Word study*

cost	expensive	cheap
honesty	honest	dishonest
flexibility	flexible	inflexible
speed	fast	slow
quality	good/high	poor/low
quantity	much/many	little/few
accuracy	accurate	inaccurate

Section B: The market environment

Part 1: Competitors

2 *Reading*

In Chart 2.4:

a. Generic competitors
b. Potato chips
c. Candy
d. Soft drinks
e. Fruit

f. Product form competitors
g. Chocolate
h. Licorice
i. Sugar drops

j. Brand competitors
k. Nestlé
l. Hershey
m. Mars

3 *Comprehension/interpretation*

3.1 It could cut the budget if not convinced of the returns.
3.2 It could cause delays in deliveries and therefore reduce demand.
3.3 It means they do not have to set up a distribution network. They can leave this side of the business to the 'experts'.

4 Language focus

4.1 Present simple

1. He skis in the Alps every winter.
2. What do you like to eat?
3. I live with my parents.
4. Do you like coffee?
5. She works very hard.
6. Do you find exercises hard?
7. Marketing plans work well.
8. Do we (always) gain market share?
9. Do you prefer the window open?
10. She loses races.

4.2 Universal conditions

1. Machines break down if they are not properly maintained.
2. Good employees leave if they are not motivated.
3. Product quality falls if there is no competition.
4. Productivity rises if an incentive scheme exists.
5. A company regresses if it is not growing.

5 Word study

Desire competitors	a luxury holiday a swimming pool
Generic competitors	a family saloon a sports car an estate car
Product form competitors	convertible turbo 2 + 2
Brand competitors	Ferrari Toyota Jaguar Porsche

Part 2: Publics

Listening tapescript

A: So, let's move on to public relations activities. What have you got planned?

B: Right, I've drawn up this table to show you what we're planning to do and who we are aiming at. In the left-hand column you can see a list of our various publics – from financial institutions down to our employees. As you know, this year is particularly important from a PR point of view. We've got a new product launch in our Health Care Business Unit and we all know that sales can be influenced very dramatically by the views of our various publics.

A: Yes, I know that. What do you have planned then?

B: Let me go through it quickly. For the banks etc. nothing special, just our usual work on the company report and the twice-yearly press conferences to coincide with the publication of our six-monthly results.

A: Okay, what about the media?

B: Well, our press relations officer is organising a press conference in a couple of months' time to coincide with the launch of Diapan. We're also trying for maximum coverage on TV and radio. For example, there's going to be a piece about the drug on the weekly medical radio programme next month.

A: I see. What about the government?

B: That's normally looked after by the legal department – you know new product safety laws and so on. However, this year we feel it's going to be important to maintain a stronger lobby in parliament. We've given Max Fisher responsibility for this area.

A: So what's he going to be doing?

B: Well, there's a lot of legislation planned on environmental issues. We need to stay informed and to let our voice be heard in parliament, so he'll be talking informally to some of the politicians interested in this area. In fact, that brings me on to the next public – pressure groups. Of course, the environmentalists are the most vocal, so Max has been briefed to act as spokesperson on these issues. We need to put across a very positive image.

A: You're right. Anything interesting on the other ones?

B: Umm, nothing new on the local community. There's still a lot of unease about the possible closure of our organic processing plant. It'll please the Greens of course but not the locals – unemployment is already high in this area. Geoff Peters, our community relations officer, is planning a series of meetings over the next five months to help reassure the local public.

A: Yes, we'll have to wait and see what the board decide. Anything else?

B: As far as the general public are concerned, I know that the corporate marketing boys are planning a TV advertising campaign. Otherwise, nothing planned. For the employees, we're sponsoring a group to go off to the Himalayas to climb some mountain – should be good for team-building.

A: All right, let me know how some of these projects develop . . .

2 *Listening*

Chart 2.5

Publics	Planned action
Financial institutions	Work on company report and six-monthly press conference
Media	Launch press conference. TV and radio – weekly medical programme
Government	Max Fisher responsibility for lobbying
Pressure groups	Max Fisher responsibility as spokesperson
Local community	Community Relations Officer to run community meetings
General public	TV advertising campaign (not PR)
Employees	Sponsor Himalayan climb

3 Comprehension/interpretation

3.1 Public relations.

3.2 To make sure the financial press write positively about the half-yearly results.

3.3 Monitor new legislation, e.g. product safety laws.

3.4 It will reduce environmental pollution.

4 Language focus

4.1 Present continuous – future reference

1. is flying
2. is installing
3. are you doing
4. is resigning

5. is moving
6. are you concentrating
7. is being implemented
8. are increasing

4.2 **Going to** – future reference

A: How's the press release *going*?

B: Oh, I haven't finished it yet. Don't worry, it'*ll be* ready on time.

A: Good. I've got a meeting with the ad agency tomorrow at 9. *Could you come*?

B: Just a moment. I'*ll look at* my diary . . .
Yes, that'*ll be* okay. What *are you going to discuss*?

A: We'*re going to talk* about the new campaign.

B: Right, I'*ll certainly be* there.

A: Great. Look, I'*m going to* lunch in half an hour. What about talking it over together first?

B: Sorry, I've got another appointment at lunch. We *could meet* later this afternoon, if you like?

A: Okay, let's say 4 o'clock in my office.

B: Fine, I'*ll be* there.

5 Word study

1. d   2. f   3. l   4. i   5. k   6. g   7. a   8. m   9. j   10. c   11. h   12. e
13. b

UNIT 3
Buyer behaviour and market segmentation

Section A: Buyer behaviour

Part 1: Consumer buyer behaviour

2   *Reading*

In Chart 3.1:

a. User   d. Decider
b. Initiator   e. Buyer
c. Influencer

Chart 3.2

Behaviour type	Product features	Product example	Marketing tasks
1. Routine response	Low-cost Frequently bought	Household detergent	Satisfy current customers Maintain quality Attract new buyers
2. Limited problem- solving	Unfamiliar brand in familiar product class	Tennis racket	Design communication programme
3. Extensive	More expensive Less familiar product class	New stereo system	To educate and to persuade

3   *Comprehension/interpretation*

3.1   This is up to you!
3.2   Food products, cleansing products.
3.3   Clothes.
3.4   Consultancy services, boats, cars.

4   *Language focus*

4.1   Scale of likelihood

1. should   5. are unlikely
2. can't/won't   6. is likely
3. will (certainly) 7. may
4. may/could   8. can't

4.2 Advice

1. Product quality is falling. You must/should/need to improve product quality.
2. Profitability is declining. You must/should/need to reduce costs.
3. Your top salespeople are leaving. You must/should/need to offer them better salaries.
4. Your deliveries are always late. You must/should/need to improve delivery times.
5. Your products are too expensive. You must/should/need to reduce prices.
6. You're growing too fast. You must/should/need to control your growth.
7. The product is not sufficiently well known. You must/should/need to extend advertising.
8. Demand exceeds supply. You must/should/need to increase production.

5 *Word study*

persuade	decide	extensive	routine	involved
suggest	choose	thorough	usual	engaged
advise	select	long-winded	regular	interested
propose	identify	complex	often	motivated
influence				

Part 2: Organisational buyer behaviour

Listening tapescript

A: Well, I suppose if we're talking about routine purchases, I'd put price top of the list and then probably delivery reliability; and I suppose I'd always keep financial strength in the top three. After all, if the supplier isn't sound financially, there's always a chance it'll go bankrupt.

B: Right, so what about new purchases of complex items?

A: I think in these cases, I'd put quality as number one criterion and then I think technical capability and thirdly delivery.

B: So you wouldn't put so much emphasis on price?

A: Well, of course, price is always important but in my opinion not so crucial in the case of large capital items.

B: Okay, thanks Mark. Peter, would you agree?

C: On the whole. Certainly, with everyday purchases, price should always be the main factor, then I'd put delivery capability followed by quality. With our more complex buying decisions, I would still put price first, then the technical capability of the firm and of course I'd have to put quality in the top three criteria again.

B: Right, thanks Peter. I'm not sure I agree entirely with either of you. If I had to choose for our routine purchases, I'd put quality first and really I'd put this top of the list for more complex items as well. The other two factors for routine purchases would be secondly delivery and thirdly price, and I suppose for the complex items, technical capability and repair service are always vital – I'm surprised neither of you mentioned repairs. If you think back to the number of times we've had to get the supplier in to fix something. So I'd put technical capability as number two and repair service number three. Somehow we've got to agree on this ranking as the MD wants me to draw up some kind of weighting system. Let's see if we can agree on the routine items?

2 Listening

Chart 3.3

	Routine purchases			Special purchases		
	A	**B**	**C**	**A**	**B**	**C**
Delivery capability	2	2	2	3		
Quality		3	1	1	3	1
Price	1	1	3		1	
Repair service						3
Technical capability				2	2	2
Financial strength	3					

3 Comprehension/interpretation

3.1 Because of the danger of a supplier going bankrupt.
3.2 Because the price differential is not so great in relative terms.
3.3 Because of the importance of receiving good and prompt service.
3.4 Because the managing director has asked for a weighting system.

4 Language focus

4.1 Conditionals

1. If demand slumped, we would have to increase advertising.
2. If we had poor weather, our sales would decrease.
3. If war broke out, we would have to scale down our production.
4. If my boss resigned, I would get his job!
5. If there was/were a strike, we would negotiate with the unions.
6. If you stopped smoking, you'd be much healthier.

4.2 **Either/neither**

1. John and Sarah both agree. Peter does too.
2. Neither Simon nor Ann agree with you. They both think you are crazy.
3. You can either leave the firm of your own free will or be fired. In any case, I want you out.
4. Neither Peter nor Roger like living in London. I don't like it either.
5. Both Marketing and Production share the same opinion about the need for higher quality. However, neither of them have come forward with any concrete proposals.

5 Word study

1. c, o, i   4. f, l, q
2. d, k, p   5. a, h, r
3. e, j, n   6. b, g, m

Section B: Market segmentation: targeting and positioning

Part 1: Targeting of segments

2 Reading

Chart 3.4

Targeting strategy	Definition	Example	Advantages	Disadvantages
Undifferentiated	Focus on what is common	Chocolate bar	Cost economies	Heavy competition Low margins
Differentiated	Target several markets	General Motors	Higher total sales	Higher costs Danger of over-segmentation
Concentrated	Target large share of small market	Sinclair	High rate of return	Higher risks Open to competition

3 Comprehension/interpretation

3.1 Many frequently purchased consumer products like detergents, bread, etc.

3.2 It is easier for a customer to stick with the name he knows rather than try out a new one.

3.3 To spread the risk.

3.4 By this stage, there is usually a lot of competition and it is more important to differentiate your product.

4 Language focus

4.1 Active versus passive

1. Market segment differences might be ignored.
2. You can design a marketing programme to appeal to most buyers.
3. Transportation costs can be kept low by a single product line.
4. You may target several market segments.
5. Differentiated marketing creates more total sales.
6. A company's base may be broadened.
7. You can find many examples of concentrated marketing.
8. The bottom end of the market was targeted by Sinclair.
9. Larger competitors may attack the segment.
10. You must consider many factors when choosing a strategy.
11. The identification of a niche would have been considered.
12. We could have added down-market products to the product range.

5 Word study

1. c   2. g   3. h   4. k   5. l   6. a   7. j   8. e   9. f   10. i   11. d   12. b

Part 2: Positioning in a segment

Listening tapescript

A: We're here today to discuss the positioning of Dentigum. I'd like to start by briefly reviewing the situation so far. Dentigum has been developed over the last two years and is now ready for production. We had hoped to be first on the market but unfortunately, as you know, Smithsons beat us to it with Dentimint – which was launched four months ago. This launch has forced us to rethink our marketing programme and especially the positioning of Dentigum in the market. What we already know is that Dentimint, our competitor, has been achieving monthly sales of around 50,000 units since its launch – so there's no doubting the potential of the market. Right, let's get down to business. I'd like to run through my preferences on positioning first. So, one possibility is that we can position it on its product attributes and benefits – in other words its anti-plaque effect and its minty taste. My own feeling is that we've lost our chance to do this – Dentimint has occupied this ground. Now, perhaps a more attractive proposition is to position it in terms of usage; in other words two or three times a day after meals – I think this could be very successful since it fits in with our research into consumer needs and behaviour. So, Peter, what do you think?

B: Well, I think there's a point you have missed. True that Smithsons have beaten us to it but I still feel we've got a very strong competitive angle – our company has been in the field of dental care for more than thirty years – some of our products have become household names – I think we should trade on this and stress the product attribute of dental care.

A: Thanks Peter. What about you Helen?

C: Well, I agree we must stress the competitive angle. I also think we can make something more out of the new product class. It's true Dentimint was launched a few months ago but I still feel we can cash in on the breakthrough product angle.

B: I think you're wrong there. Any more publicity about the product class will benefit our competitors not us. We've got to stress our track record in the dental field, not theirs.

A: So neither of you favour the usage angle? I'm surprised. I think you haven't really understood the position. It's no good trying to attract Dentimint buyers away – we've got to build our own customer base with a clear message which gives our product a very different identity.

2 Listening

Chart 3.5

Positioning	Speaker 1	Speaker 2	Speaker 3
Product attributes		✓	✓
Usage	✓		
Competitive advantage		✓	✓

3 *Comprehension/interpretation*

3.1   2 years.
3.2   4 months ago.
3.3   50,000.
3.4   This positioning has not been used by the competition.
3.5   30 years.
3.6   This will benefit the competition.

4 *Language focus*

4.1   Present perfect versus past simple

1. We *reached* our targets last year.
2. Sales *have fallen* since the beginning of June.
3. Contracts *have been signed* but work *hasn't begun* yet.
4. The marketing department *has recruited* two new assistants so far this year.
5. We *started* the advertising campaign last month and since then sales *have rocketed*.
6. Our research *was carried out* last year but I still *haven't seen* the results.
7. Turnover *has risen* dramatically since we *were founded*.
8. We *expected* a fall in profits last year as our costs nearly *doubled*.
9. We *have* already *sold* more units this year than we *did* in the whole of last year.
10. He *felt* we should *not have taken on* so many salespeople last year.

4.2   Present perfect continuous

1. Liverpool has won all its matches this season.
2. Liverpool has been playing very well this season.
3. We have sold 250 units this quarter.
4. Our sales strategy has been working very well.
5. It has been raining all day.
6. It has been cold since March.
7. He has been ill for two days.
8. I've been trying to telephone you all day.
9. We have survived the competition.
10. Prices have fallen from 15p a unit to 12p.

5 *Word study*

1. track record
2. in the field
3. breakthrough
4. a household name
5. trade on
6. beat them to
7. build a customer base
8. make something

UNIT 4
Products

Section A: Product type and mix decisions

Part 1: Branding decisions

2 *Reading*

In Chart 4.2:

a. Manufacturer
b. Private label
c. Both labels

d. Individual
e. Family
f. Separate family
g. Company trade name

3 *Comprehension/interpretation*

3.1 This usually means the product is cheaper because no money has been spent on advertising.

3.2 The manufacturers' label is associated with mass production whereas the private label suggests exclusivity.

3.3 They have wanted to segment the market and position different products with their own identity in different segments.

3.4 Up to you!

4 *Language focus*

4.1 Question formation: **wh-** questions

1. How often do you go shopping?
2. Why do you go shopping?
3. Who usually does the shopping?
4. What type of products do you buy in a supermarket?
5. How much do you spend weekly?
6. Which products do you prefer?
7. Which types of branded products do you buy?
8. How much extra are you prepared to pay?
9. How did you hear of the product?
10. What do you think of this product?

4.2 Question formation: **yes/no** questions

1. Do you enjoy shopping?
2. Do you shop in large supermarkets?
3. Do you think shopping services have improved?
4. Do you spend about three hours shopping a week?

5. Do you use a mint toothpaste?
6. Have you heard of Dentigum?
7. Have you tried Dentigum?
8. Would you like to try some?
9. Did you like it?
10. Would you like to buy some?

5 Word study

1. c   2. e   3. d   4. a   5. b

6 Transfer

B: Use the information below to answer your partner's questions. Try to reach a decision about branding.

Product	Anti-wrinkle cream for men
Core product – benefits	softens and moisturises the skin on men's faces
Tangible product – features package quality branding	white, unscented, non-greasy cream pump-action, masculine style container up-market, well researched, high price ?
Manufacturer	very well known company in women's toiletries. They use family name: 'No.6' for full range. Products sold in pharmacies and fashion stores throughout the world

Part 2: Product line decisions

Listening tapescript

I'd like briefly to review our product development over the last ten years and then move on to some recommendations for the future.

As you know, we started back in 1980 with one product – this was English language training. Under this category we offered two basic services: individual and group training. The language training has developed over the years so that we now offer a range of languages in addition to English – the main ones are French, German, Spanish and Italian. In terms of product depth, we haven't extended the basic formula of either individual or group training.

Right. In 1985 we extended our product mix when we started a new division – communication training. This line has developed steadily so that we now cover three major communication skills areas. These are: effective presentations, effective meetings and interviewing skills. In terms of depth, all training is offered on a group basis but we distinguish between *public seminars* – open through various institutes to the employees of any company, and *company seminars* which are for closed groups from one company.

Finally, two years ago, we developed a new product line under the title of management training. Under this heading, the product line includes leadership skills training, team-building and decision-making. At the moment these products are only offered on a company basis for closed groups.

So that gives you an idea of our product spread. I'd now like to outline the potential areas of development as we see it. In terms of product mix, one option we could go for is to set up a new training division offering information technology training. The sort of product line we could envisage here would include database management training, word-processing skills and distributed information systems.

A second area of development might be to stretch one of the product lines to include additional training products. For example, under communication training, I know some of our staff feel we should be developing negotiating skills training.

Alternatively, we could focus on some of our more profitable training areas such as leadership skills and extend the range offered under one product item. Here we could be thinking of selling public seminars as well as the company seminars.

2 Listening

In Chart 4.3:

a. Communication training   b. Management training

In Chart 4.4:

a. German   d. Meetings   f. Team-building
b. Spanish   e. Interviewing   g. Decision-making
c. Italian

In Chart 4.5:

a. Closed   b. Open   c. Closed

In Chart 4.6:

a. IT training   b. Negotiation skills   c. Public seminars

3 Comprehension/interpretation

3.1   A public seminar is open to all; a company seminar is closed to the general public.
3.2   Up to you!
3.3   Probably product mix developments.

4 Language focus

4.1   Past reference

1. He's been off work for three months.
2. He ought to have retired a year ago.
3. She's been with the company since it began.
4. It's hard to gauge success over/in just two months.
5. She left the country at 1400 on Tuesday.
6. We didn't receive the delivery on/in time.
7. At the beginning of the year, prospects looked good.
8. There was a downturn in the middle of March.
9. Since 1980, our prices have been falling.
10. We installed a new computer network two years ago.

4.2   Scale of likelihood

1. d   3. b, h   5. g
2. a, e   4. f   6. c, i

5   *Word study*

5.1   negotiable
5.2   extensive
5.3   leadership
5.4   distinction
5.5   presentation
5.6   production/productivity
5.7   profitable
5.8   negotiators

Section B: Product development decisions

Part 1: New product development

2   *Reading*

Chart 4.7

Strategies	Examples	Advantages	Disadvantages
Acquisition	P&G/R-V Thomson/RCA Nestlé/Rowntree	Cheaper Less risky Quick and easy access	Govt restrictions High initial price
Me-toos	Tandy Sanyo Compaq	Quick Cheap to develop Can offer more proven market	Late entry Strong competition
Revivals	Ivory soap Black Jack	'New' at low cost	Backward-looking

3   *Comprehension/interpretation*

3.1   Because of anti-trust/monopoly laws.
3.2   Pepsi-Cola
3.3   New health-conscious market.

4 Language focus

4.1 Connectors 1

1. Despite
2. Although
3. In addition
4. However
5. thus
6. Moreover

4.2 Connectors 2

These are only model answers; others are possible.

1. Although sales have decreased, profits have increased.
2. One advantage is that you have instant access to the market. In addition/Moreover, you can deliberately undercut your competitors.
3. (As/Because) we were making a loss, (so/therefore) we withdrew from the market.
4. The product sold well in the South. However, in the North, the results were disastrous.
5. We promoted the product at the point of sale while/whereas our competitors used mass advertising.

5 Word study

Success	Old products	Market penetration
to succeed	dead	to move into
to reverse the decline	tarnished	to strengthen your hold
to rocket	to rejuvenate	to ride on the coattails
	to rise again	to enter
	dying	
	to revive	
Acquisition	**Payment**	
to gobble up	to cough up	
to merge	to pay out	
to take over	to fork out	
to obtain		
to absorb		

Part 2: Product life cycle

Listening tapescript

What I'd like to do today is to describe the AZ100's history so far in terms of sales and profitability and then move on to suggest ways in which we can maintain present sales and profit levels over the next ten years.

So, to go back to the beginning – the AZ100 was originally conceived in 1975 by Dr Rubin and his research team – they worked on developing a prototype for two years and finally we were ready to launch it in 1977. Our investment costs reached their peak in 1978 when we had negative profitability on the project of $4 million. As planned, the launch phase lasted about one year and sales began to climb so that by the end of '79 they had reached $5 million and at the same time we began to see a profit. During the next five years the sales rocketed to reach $20 million by 1985. At this stage profits stood at $3 million. After '85 our sales continued to rise until they reached a peak of $25 million in 1988. Meanwhile profits declined slightly to $2.5 million at the same time as we invested heavily in advertising to meet the competition. Since '88, sales have levelled off around $25 million and profits have continued to decrease slightly and now stand at just over $2 million.

Right, so that brings you up to date. Now as you can see see on the graph here – the dotted lines representing a projection – in the normal line of events we could expect to phase out the product in 1995 when sales are forecast to drop to around $10 million and profits have nearly fallen to zero.

However, I'd like you to consider the following strategy. We have already done all the research and testing on an updated version of the AZ100. We've called it the AZ1000. We could launch this product within six months at a premium price – in this way we can segment the market – leave our existing product to decline gradually in the low-margin mass market – while we promote heavily the AZ1000 in a sector where typical profit margins are in the region of 40 per cent. I project, if we do this, that we will achieve sales figures of $5 million by 1995 and can expect profits around $2 million.

2 Listening

Chart 4.8

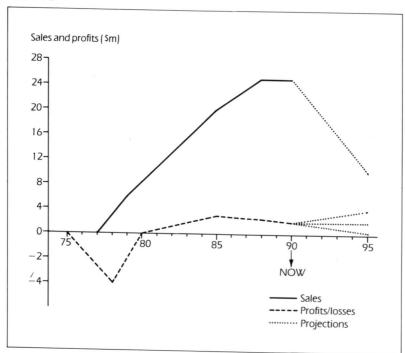

3 Comprehension/interpretation

3.1 Part 1: Sales and profitability of AZ100.
    Part 2: Ways of maintaining sales and profitability.
3.2 Because of high initial investment costs.
3.3 Investment in advertising.
3.4 At a high (value-added) price.

4 Language focus

4.1 Describing graphs

1. b   2. c   3. d   4. f   5. g   6. e   7. a

4.2 Describing trends

1. g   2. h   3. b   4. j   5. c   6. d   7. f   8. i   9. a   10. e

5 Word study

a. slow growth   e. few   i. product awareness
b. peak levels   f. many rivals j. rising
c. negative   g. defend share k. improved
d. laggards   h. falling

UNIT 5
Pricing

Section A: Factors to consider when setting prices

Part 1: Analysis of price–demand relationship

2 Reading

a. Figure 5.3
b. Figure 5.2
c. Figure 5.5
d. Figure 5.6
e. Figure 5.4
f. Figure 5.1

3 Comprehension/interpretation

3.1 Standard demand curve
3.2 Prestige goods demand curve
3.3 Demand curve for motor oil
3.4 Effect of non-price factors on demand
3.5 Inelastic demand
3.6 Elastic demand

4 Language focus

4.1 Cause and effect – verbs

1. Price increases can lead to a fall in demand.
2. A sales decrease may result in redundancies.
3. Doubling of the advertising budget should lead to a sales increase.
4. A gradual decline in the market sector has resulted in a fall in share prices.
5. A reduction in staff salaries will lead to a decline in staff motivation.

NOTE: Other combinations are possible.

4.2 Cause and effect – if clauses, etc.

1. If the company raises wages, production costs will increase.
2. The more the production costs increase, the higher prices will rise.
3. If prices rise, demand will fall.
4. The more demand falls, the more sales will decrease.
5. If sales decrease, production will fall.

5 Word study

1. c   2. d   3. b   4. g   5. h   6. m   7. n   8. e   9. j   10. i
11. f   12. k   13. a   14. l

Part 2: Pricing decisions

Listening tapescript

A: We're here to make a decision on the launch price of Apollo – our new anti-wrinkle cream for men. David has already presented his price–demand analysis and suggested a retail price of around $12. This would maximise sales around the 40,000 unit mark. What we need to do now is to look at this figure once again in relation to our costs, target profits, perceived value to the customers and also the going-rate in the market.

B: Excuse me, what do you mean by going rate?

A: Well, basically what our competitors are charging for similar products.

B: I see.

A: Okay, let's take costs first. Our variable costs are reckoned to be $2 per unit, our fixed costs in the plant stand at $160,000, so the manufacturer's cost is $6.

C: Sorry, you're going too fast for me. How did you get to that total cost.

A: Very simple really. I added the variable cost to the fixed costs divided by the unit sales – 160,000 divided by 40,000 – that gives us 4 – 4 plus 2 is 6.

C: Of course, I've got it now.

A: Now the retailers will want to mark this product up by at least 50 per cent – so that means our manufacturer's price to the retailers has got to be $8 if we are to end up with a $12 price tag in the shops.

C: I'm sorry, can you go over that again?

A: Sure, I'll put it on the flip chart. Our cost is $6 – the retailer wants a 50 per cent mark-up, so if we sell to them for $8, they can mark it up for a further $4 – 50 per cent to give us our target price of $12. Is that clear?

C: Yes, I think I see that now. If I have understood you correctly, that only gives us a margin of $2 per unit.

A: That's right. It's not enough. Let's look at the perceived value. All our market research shows that this is a high quality product – I'm sure $12 to the buyer is not the limit.

D: Well, as I said, I think it is the limit if we are going for optimum sales. Certainly some consumers would be happy to pay more but $12 is certainly pitched just about right to attract as many as possible.

A: Okay David. Let's look at the going rates. Women's anti-wrinkle cream is retailing at around $16 a unit. Correct me if I'm wrong?

D: No, that's absolutely right.

A: The only other male anti-wrinkle cream is on the market at around $14.

D: That's true but I think you're missing the point. Artemis, our direct competitor, retails for $14 but the sales figure is around 20,000. As you know, we've based all our target and profit analysis on achieving a fairly rapid rate of return – that means going for 40,000 sales at the lower price of $12.

2 Listening

a. $12
b. 40,000
c. $2 per unit
d. $4 per unit
e. 50% ($4)
f. $2
g. $14–16

3 Comprehension/interpretation

3.1 Market price.
3.2 Variable cost per unit + fixed cost per unit.
3.3 As a high quality product.
3.4 To achieve a fairly rapid rate of return.

4 Language focus

4.1 Asking for clarification

A: The central problem is cannibalism.
B: *Excuse me, what do you mean by* cannibalism?
A: Well, basically our new product taking sales away from our existing product. *Is that clear?*
B: Yes, I see what you *mean.*
A: Now we have to weigh up the added sales and margin we gain and balance that against our losses.
B: *I'm sorry, could you go over that more* slowly?
A: Of course. Well in order to calculate the real profit we gain from the launch of the ZX21 we must take into account the lost sales on the ZX20.
B: *I see.*
A: Good, now this model here plots the projected sales of the ZX21 over the first twelve months against the projected continued sales of the ZX20. As you can see, the gap widens quite dramatically.
A: If I *understand you correctly*, you're *saying* this gap represents lost sales?
B: No, it's not quite that simple.

NOTE: Other expressions are possible.

4.2 Confirming and correcting statements

1. That's right.
2. Yes, that's true.
3. No, that's not true, actually.
4. That's absolutely right.
5. You're right there.
6. No, that's not the case.

NOTE: Other expressions are possible.

5 Word study

1. $40
2. $14
3. $40,000
4. $6 + 4 = 10$
5. $\dfrac{160,000}{40,000} = 4$

6. $15,000 - 5,000 = 10,000$
7. $8 \times 20 = 160$
8. ½
9. ¼
10. ⅞

Section B: Pricing strategies

Part 1: Price wars

2 *Reading*

In Chart 5.6:

$g \rightarrow c \rightarrow a \rightarrow h \rightarrow f \rightarrow k \rightarrow b \rightarrow d \rightarrow i \rightarrow j \rightarrow e \rightarrow l$

3 *Comprehension/interpretation*

3.1 To gain market share.
3.2 Because of a strong dollar and lower manufacturing costs.
3.3 No.
3.4 Because of a weaker dollar.

4 *Language focus*

4.1 Past simple (irregular verbs)

1. We fought off the challenge from our competitors.
2. We cut our prices dramatically.
3. They outsold us in all sectors of the market.
4. We might have lost our dominant position.
5. We saw a gradual erosion of our position.
6. Komatsu ate into our share of the market.
7. We brought forward our monthly meeting.
8. They bought into the company by acquiring ordinary shares.
9. We took market share from our competitors.
10. The whole market swelled significantly.

4.2 Subordinate clauses

1. Caterpillar, by reducing prices dramatically, regained market share.
2. Komatsu, using a low-price strategy, entered the market.
3. The construction equipment market, which has been dominated by Caterpillar for many years, has now become fragmented.
4. As prices fell, due to heavy discounting in the sector, profit margins narrowed.
5. Smaller competitors, whose margins were squeezed, were forced out of the market.
6. Price, which is a major factor is some markets, can be ignored in this market.

5 *Word study*

5.1
1. rises   2. raised   3. rose   4. raise   5. has risen

5.2

1. bloody battle	5. slashed costs	(9. peaceful coexistence)
2. major weapon	6. driven to the brink of ruin	
3. ruthlessly	7. the challenger	
4. fought back	8. fierce	

Part 2: Price adjustment strategies

Listening tapescript

A: Murphy Rogers, can I help you?

B: Could you put me through to Mr Stevens in the Sales Department?

A: Certainly. Who's calling, sir?

B: This is Geoff Denny from Garfield Wholesale Electricals.

A: Just a moment, Mr Denny, I'll put you through . . .

C: Stevens speaking.

B: Hello, this is Geoff Denny.

C: Geoff, how are you?

B: Fine. The reason I'm phoning is we need to sort out a final price on the coffee-machines.

C: Of course; what did we quote you?

B Well, you gave us a unit price of £20.

C: That's right. Are you happy with that?

B: It depends. We intend to purchase about 150 to 200 a month. So we were wondering what sort of quantity discount you can offer us.

C: I see. Just a moment. I'll get my tables . . . Well, at an order quantity of 200, we would be willing to offer you a 10 per cent discount.

B: So that'll bring down the unit price to £18.

C: That's right . . . a very favourable price.

B: Uhum . . . What about larger quantities – for example, what about putting in a quarterly order of around 500?

C: Well, I don't have any figures for those sorts of quantities, but I know we've got one customer who gets 15 per cent on 500.

B: I see, so that would be £17 per unit?

C: Correct, I'd have to confirm that.

B: Sure, I understand.

C: There's another point to mention which is payment terms. Would you be interested in a discount for early payment?

B: What sort of figure do you have in mind?

C: Well, we are prepared to offer 2 per cent for payment within fifteen days. Our normal terms are thirty days.

B: Interesting. I'll have to get back to you on that.

C: Right.

B: There's just one more point. As you know, this is going to be a new line for us. We wondered if you might offer some kind of promotional allowance on the first order?

C: Well, we don't normally do that.

B: It's just that we could put more aside to promote the product to our retailers and that could well mean bigger sales.

C: Yes, I see that. Maybe we could discuss an additional discount on the first 500 of around 2 per cent.

B: That doesn't sound very generous.

C: Well I'm sure you'll understand we've got our margins to protect.

B: Of course. Look, I've got a meeting now. Perhaps you could let me know whether you can do any better than that and let me have all the prices in writing.

C: I'll certainly do that and I'll get a letter in the post this afternoon.

B: Thanks. I must be going. I'll speak to you soon then.

C: Right, we'll be in touch. Goodbye.
B: Bye.

2   Listening

In Chart 5.7:

a. £20   b. 10%   c. 15%   d. 2%   e. 2%

3   Comprehension/interpretation

In Chart 5.8

a. Geoff Denny
b. Mr Stevens
c. To agree a final price for coffee machines
d. Quotation in writing

4   Language focus

4.1   Telephoning

A: Rogers Electronics
B: Good afternoon. This is Max Roberts from Excel Marketing. Could you put me through to your Sales Department?
A: I'm sorry. I didn't catch your name.
B: Its Roberts.
A: Thank you, Mr Roberts. I'll try to put you through . . . I'm afraid the line's busy at the moment. Will you hold?
B: Yes, I'll hang on.
A: Right, Mr Roberts, I'm putting you through now.
C: Sales. Dickens speaking.
B: Hello, my name's Max Roberts. I'm from Excel Marketing. The reason I'm calling is that we are carrying out a market survey . . .
C: Just a moment, Mr Roberts. I'll put you through to our market research assistant . . . I'm sorry, he's out at the moment. Would you like to call back?
B: Certainly, perhaps you could give me his extension number.
C: Yes, it's 453. His name is Holden. John Holden.
B: Thanks for your help.
C: You're welcome. Bye.
B: Goodbye.

4.2   Offering and requesting

A: We were wondering if you could offer us a discount?
B: Well, we could certainly discuss it.
A: What sort of discount were you thinking of?
B: We would be willing to offer you 2 per cent.
A: I'm afraid that's much lower than we're expecting.
B: Well, I'm sure you'll understand that's a reasonable offer.
A: Yes, but, considering our excellent relationships, I'm sure you could offer a bit more?
B: Perhaps we could consider ½ per cent?

A: We were thinking more in terms of 5 per cent.
B: I'm afraid that's far too high.
A: Well, Perhaps we could say 3½ per cent?
B: I'm sorry, that's still too high.
A: I'm sure I don't have to point out what a valuable customer we are?
B: Certainly, we're very aware of that. Perhaps we could settle on 3 per cent?
A: That sounds reasonable.
B: Good. Let's leave it at that, shall we?

5 *Word study*

1. j   c
2. b   h
3. a   i
4. f   d
5. g   e

6 *Transfer*

B: You work for a supplier of electrical goods. You will receive a telephone call from A. S/he will want to negotiate the best price possible for a regular order of hairdryers. Here are some figures for your telephone call. Don't give too much away!

Hairdryer prices:

Unit price:	£10
Quantity discounts:	10% 100+
	15% 200+
	20% 500+
Cash discounts:	2% for payment within 10 days
	(normal terms: 30 days)
Seasonal discounts:	10% (January) – to clear old stock
Promotional allowances:	not usual but could be negotiated

UNIT 6
Placing

Section A: Distribution channels

Part 1: Distribution channels: types and organisation

2 *Reading*

In Chart 6.1:

a. Corporate VMS
b. Contractual VMS
c. Administered VMS
d. Wholesaler voluntary chains
e. Franchise organisations
f. Manufacturer-sponsored wholesale franchise
g. Service firm-sponsored retailer franchise system

3 *Comprehension/interpretation*

3.1 They provide stronger leadership and improved performance
3.2 (i)   It enables independent retailers to compete with large chain organisations.
     (ii) They can cut out the wholesaler and even move into producton.
     (iii) They provide a relatively cheap way to set up a network without involving the
           franchiser in the day-to-day management of the franchisee.
3.3 Manufacturers (especially of top brands).

4 *Language focus*

4.10 Quantity and amount

1. We sell any type you like.
2. We are involved in all the stages of wine production and distribution.
3. We have studied every/each step in the distribution process.
4. We studied all of the major wine producers. Each of them has some advantage.
5. You asked me if we can supply any/every retailer in the north of England. In fact, we can
   reach any/everyone within a thirty mile radius of Newcastle.
6. We are involved in every aspect of wine distribution.
7. All major wine producers have suffered from the recession.

4.2 Noun compounds

1. A service firm-sponsored retailer franchise system.
2. A manufacturer-funded wholesale distribution network.
3. A retailer-run customer cooperative.
4. An industry-financed competitor market survey.
5. A government-supported employers' association.
6. A bankruptcy-threatened employees' union.

5 Word study

employment	employer	employee
franchising	franchiser	franchisee
licensing	licenser	licensee
leasing	lessor	lesee
buying/selling	vendor	buyer/purchaser

Part 2: Managing channels

Listening tapescript

A: Hello, Giorgio. How are you?

B: Fine, nice to hear from you.

A: I was just phoning to see how things are going?

B: Well, not bad. I think the monthly figures as a whole should be just a little below target.

A: Really, I thought this was going to be a good month?

B: Yes, in a way it has been but you know your targets are very ambitious.

A: You seemed perfectly happy about them when we set them together at the beginning of the year.

B: Yes, well perhaps I was a bit over-optimistic. The market's becoming very competitive and I really haven't got time to get round to see all the customers.

A: I see. Does that mean you need help?

B: No, no, its just a question of giving up more time.

A: Exactly. Let's just go through the product line and see where we stand.

B: Okay. Just a moment. I'll get the latest figures . . . So on the XR50 it looks like we'll hit 220 – that's above target!

A: Good. We only set 200 for this month, didn't we?

B: That's right. The XR100 is not moving so well. We'll probably shift about 150 units.

A: Oh . . . that's rather disappointing. That's way below target. We were aiming for 300.

B: Yes, I know. As I said, I really haven't got the time to push this one. The customers are really widely dispersed.

A: All right. We'll come back to that. What about the XR120?

B: That's just about on target. Around 80 this month.

A: That's fine. As you know, the profit margin on the XR120 is very good. Anyway you seem to be saying you need more help on the middle of the range product?

B: No, not exactly, it's more a question of . . .

2 Listening

Chart 6.2

Product	Actual results	Target
XR50	220	200
XR100	150	300
XR120	80	80

3 Comprehension/interpretation

3.1 At the beginning of the year.
3.2 No, they did it together.
3.3 The market's become very competitive and he hasn't time to see all the customers.
3.4 The customers are widely dispersed.
3.5 Because the profit margin is good on this product.

4 Language focus

4.1 Responding positively and negatively

1. c   2. b   3. b   4. c   5. a   6. c

4.2 Modifiers/softeners

1. *Perhaps* he's *a bit* too ambitious.
2. Let's *just* go through your figures.
3. *In a way*, we're growing *a bit* too fast.
4. *In a way*, he's much too direct.
5. *Perhaps*, we are *a little bit* late.
6. *Perhaps*, your products are *a bit* expensive.
7. I'm *a bit* unsure of your liquidity.
8. *In a way*, that's not good enough.

5 Word study

1. just a little below target
2. just about on target
3. way above target
4. optimistic . . . set/fixed
5. realistic . . . set/fixed
6. (over)-pessimistic . . . set/fixed

Section B: Wholesaling and retailing

Part 1: Wholesaler marketing decisions

2 Reading

Chart 6.3

Precision areas	Present characteristics	Needs
Target markets	Serve too many customers	To define their market To identify more profitable customers; to discourage less profitable ones
Assortment	Too wide a range	To carry fewer lines, less stock; identify more profitable lines
Pricing	20% mark-up (3% margin)	To vary pricing strategy
Promotion	Haphazard promotion policy	To develop promotional strategy Use image-making techniques
Place	Located in low-rent, low-tax areas – do not invest in physical setting	To study automated materials handling

3 Comprehension/interpretation

3.1 By requiring larger orders and adding surcharges to smaller ones.

3.2 When they can increase sales.

3.3 Because they don't have contact with the end-user, therefore they don't see the value of investment in this area.

3.4 More efficient management of stock-handling, accounting, billing, inventory control and forecasting.

4 Language focus

4.1 Present simple versus present continuous

1. Usually we *destock* at this time of year. This year we *are stocking up*.
2. Wholesalers generally *are not interested* in their physical location. However, this *is changing*. Some companies *are repositioning* themselves through promotion and investment.
3. Inventory control *remains* absolutely essential but fewer stock lines *mean* the wholesaler can *direct* his attention more to the commercial side.
4. In my opinion, Ecom Distribution *is making* a mistake by relocating to outside town.
5. Many wholesalers *make* the mistake of handling too many lines.
6. We *are moving* our premises in order to reduce transportation costs.
7. If transportation costs *come down*, we will be able to invest in automated handling.
8. He always *talks/is always talking* about investing but he never *does* anything.

4.2 Too/enough

1. That's not expensive enough.
2. There's too little investment.
3. There's not enough advertising.
4. It's not simple enough.
5. We use too little automation.
6. We promote too little.
7. We're too unimaginative.

5 Word study

1. g	2. b	3. d/e	4. b	5. g/b	6. c	7. g (all other combinations are possible)
8. a	9. f	10. c	11. a			

Part 2: Order processing

Listening tapescript

A: Klondike Electronics

B: Could I speak to someone in the sales department?

A: Just a moment, I'll put you through.

C: Susan Kerly speaking. Can I help you?

B: This is George Roberts from McKenzies. I'm phoning about our order for the XR500s.

C: Right, Mr Roberts. Can you just give me the order number?

B: Yes, it's MK/40XR500/290

C: . . . Right I've got it. So what's the problem?

B: The problem is they haven't arrived.

C: Oh . . .

B: They were due on March 1st. We telephoned last week, must have been the 10th and were promised them the next day – the 11th. Well, it's now the 16th and there's still no sign.

C: I see. That's very strange. I know our orders for XR500s are usually despatched at the end of every week. Look, can I call you back?

B: Please do. My number's 0432 810352 extension 24.

C: Right. I'll phone you back in the next ten minutes.

B: George Roberts speaking.

C: Mr Roberts, this is Susan Kerly from Klondike.

B: Ah right. I hope you've got some good news for me.

C: First of all, I must apologise. Your order had got mixed up with another customer's. I've arranged for a truck to go down and pick it up this afternoon. It should be with you later this afternoon.

B: Good. While you're on the phone perhaps you can make a note of a new order?

C: Certainly

B: We need twenty of the XR30s as soon as possible.

C: Let me just check the stock figures . . . Yes, that's no problem. We should be able to get them to you by the beginning of next week.

B: You couldn't manage any earlier?
C: I'll do my best. At the earliest on Friday this week though.
B: Okay. Thanks for your help.
C: You're welcome and once again I'm sorry about the other order.
B: Well, hopefully it won't happen again. Bye.
C: Bye.

2 Listening

Chart 6.4

	Order no.	Product	Quantity	Delivery due	Action
1st order	MK/40XR500/290	XR500	–	1 March	Phone back
2nd order	–	XR30	20	Beg. of next week	Try for this Friday

3 Comprehension/interpretation

Up to you!

4 Language focus

4.1 Time prepositions

1. in
2. on/by on/by
3. on, at
4. at, in/by
5. by/at
6. in, Ø/by

4.2 Telephoning

A: Hello, this is Geoff Peters, I'm phoning about the conference.
B: Hello, Mr Peters. This is Martine Donaugh. How can I help you?
A: Well you promised to send me details of travel and accommodation.
B: Oh, I am sorry. You haven't received it then?
A: No, and the conference starts tomorrow.
B: Of course. Look, can I check the file and call you back?
A: Fine, have you got my number?
B: I'm sure I have, but just in case, I'll take it again.
A: Its 031-465-389, extension 26.
B: Right, I've got that. I'll call you back in a few minutes. Goodbye.
A: Goodbye.

5 Word study

1. supplier
2. delivery
3. supplying
4. supplier, delivery, despatched
5. despatch
6. Suppliers, deliver

6 *Transfer*

B: You represent Klondike Electronics. You were expecting a delivery of electric irons from overseas two months ago. The manufacturer has severe production problems. You are trying to find a new source/supplier for these irons.

UNIT 7
Promotion

Section A: Communication and advertising

Part 1: Choosing the message

2 *Reading*

In Chart 7.1:

a. Rational	d. Conclusion drawing	g. Written	j. Expertise
b. Emotional	e. One- or two-sided	h. Spoken	k. Trustworthiness
c. Moral	f. Order of presentation	i. Non-verbal	l. Likeability

3 *Comprehension/interpretation*

Some suggestions:

  (i)   Content: rational
        Structure: conclusion-drawing
        Format: spoken and non-verbal
        Source: expertise

  (ii) Content: emotional
        Structure: order of presentation, leading to strongest argument
        Format: spoken + non-verbal (for TV campaign)
        Source: likeability

  (iii) Content: moral
        Structure: two-sided argument
        Format: written
        Source: expertise and trustworthiness

4 *Language focus*

4.1   Verb + preposition

  1. We are looking *for* a message which really appeals *to* the audience. So far we haven't found one.
  2. One strong emotional appeal nowadays is the environment. Looking *after* the environment well carries a strong appeal.
  3. We can't decide *on* the message format. We need to look *for* a strong non-verbal approach.
  4. People tend to look *up* to expert figures such as doctors.
  5. We were thinking *of* doing the ad on television.
  6. He insisted *on* using a balanced argument to present the product.
  7. I was very annoyed *at/by* the simplicity of the arguments. Consumers like to think *about* the product.

8. If you look *up* the word in the dictionary, it means all communication which is non-verbal.
9. Have you heard *of* Professor Stell? He's very well known in his field.
10. We've looked *into* the question of hiring professional actors. It's much too expensive.

4.2   Verb + infinitive/verb + (preposition) + **ing**

1. He accused me *of selling* my talent cheaply.
2. They liked *to watch/watching* cowboy films.
3. He insisted *on talking* all the way through the film.
4. We were *prevented from* entering the building.
5. He hated *listening* to the radio.
6. We are very keen *on listening* to classical music.
7. They loved *to play/playing* music together.
8. They attempted *to sell* the film rights.
9. We were forced *to rely* on an unknown actress.
10. We were stopped *from demonstrating* outside the hall.

5   Word study

1. e, j, o, s	4. c, h, l, r
2. b, g, k	5. d, i (could be 1 in sense of 'clever'), n
3. a, f, m, p, t	

Part 2: Choosing the media

Listening tapescript

(A = Sheila, B = John, C = Pete, D = Mike)

A: Right, before we set a budget for this campaign, I'd like to hear your suggestions on media. John, would you like to start?

B: What I suggest we do is go for ten slots on TV backed by more regular exposure on commercial radio.

A: Okay. That's brief and to the point. Pete, do you agree?

C: Well, I'd agree on the media type. There's no doubt that TV and radio will reach our target audience. I'm not sure about the frequency. I think we are going to need many more slots on TV to ensure the sort of exposure we're aiming for. I'd recommend we think in terms of twenty peak-time slots over an initial three-week period.

D: I think you're both wrong. Okay, teenagers watch a lot of TV and listen to commercial radio. But that's the very reason why the commercials don't really reach them – they see or hear too many. I think we should seriously consider putting glossy ads in youth magazines and maybe do some outdoor advertising. We're going to have to increase our sales budget for selling into the department stores, sports and shoe shops. We're not going to have too much over for advertising.

C: Come on Mike. We may hit the right people with magazines but we're not going to hit enough.

D: I disagree. Word of mouth is what counts amongst teenagers. We know we'll reach the right people, we know we'll get their attention in the magazines and tied in with effective sales promotion at the stores, we'll get the initial sales. Once their friends see them wearing them, we'll get the followers. Maybe we could consider TV to gain – to establish a brand image but I don't think we need that now.

B: That's where you're wrong. These kids only care about image. Without an image-making TV ad, the product's dead.

A: Right, that's interesting. I propose we think in terms of launch advertising on TV – that'll help with the sales push to the department stores – then supported by magazine ads as Mike has suggested. I don't think we'll bother with radio. Okay, let's look at how much that is going to cost us.

2 Listening

Chart 7.2

	TV	Radio	Newspapers	Magazines	Outdoor
John	✓	✓			
Pete	✓	✓			
Mike				✓	✓
Sheila	✓			✓	

3 Comprehension/interpretation

1. 1 = TV   2 = newspapers   3 = outdoor   4 = magazines   5 = radio
2. 1 = outdoor   2 = newspapers   3 = magazines   4 = radio   5 = TV
3. 1 = magazines   2 = newspapers   3 = radio   4 = TV   5 = outdoor
4. 1 = TV   2 = magazines   3 = newspapers   4 = radio   5 = outdoor
5. 1 = magazines   2 = newspapers   3 = radio   4 = TV   5 = outdoor

NOTE: These are only suggestions; discuss specific product advertising and where it is best placed.

4 Language focus

4.1 Suggest/recommend

1. I propose investing/we invest in TV advertising.
2. He suggests using/we use outside advertising.
3. They recommend we forget/forgetting about radio.
4. We might consider placing print ads in prestige magazines.
5. He advises us to reduce our advertising budget.
6. I'd like to suggest we look at/looking at new media.
7. We (would) strongly recommend you study the TV ratings.
8. Let's think about targeted ads in trade journals.

4.2 Emphasis – word order

1. What we should do is target this age group very carefully.
2. What we need to do is to concentrate on direct sales.
3. What they must do is reduce their advertising budget.

4. What I recommend you do is try to reach the department stores.
5. What we feel you have missed is an opportunity.
6. What they thought was that we had spent too much on outdoor advertising.
7. What he expected us to do was to hire a professional singer.
8. What I propose to do is limit your advertising to radio.

5 Word study

1. d   2. g   3. a   4. j   5. f   6. h   7. b   8. i   9. e   10. c

Section B: Personal selling

Part 1: Selling styles

2 Reading

Chart 7.3

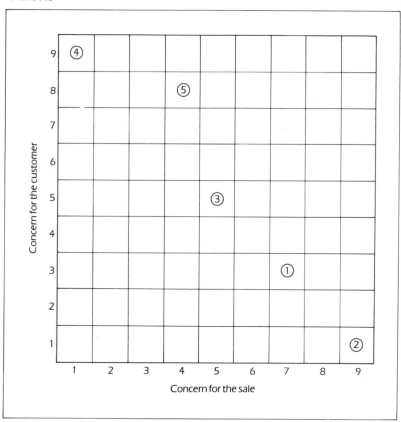

3   Comprehension/interpretation

These answers could be disputed!

3.1   Type 3
3.2   Type 4
3.3   Type 2
3.4   Type 5

4   Language focus

4.1   Similarity and difference

1. Selling techniques differ depending on the type of customer and product.
2. There is a big difference between selling a car and selling a consultancy service.
3. All customers are similar in one sense. They are all interested in value for money.
4. Selling styles differ from one country to another. A door-to-door salesman in Japan behaves differently from one in the US.
5. We can distinguish between two distinct styles: the product-oriented and the customer-oriented.
6. There are many similarities in selling services. Concern for the customer is common to all services.

4.2   Reflexive pronouns

1. We congratulated ourselves. Nobody else said anything.
2. The problem with selling yourself is that there's nobody else who can replace you.
3. We were invited to a sales conference in Harrogate.
4. Where's you invitation? – I haven't got one. I invited myself.
5. New products rarely sell themselves. You have to inform the market.
6. One shouldn't only think of oneself. There are others to consider.
7. I (myself) would like to go home. My wife wants to stay.
8. Cars, in themselves, should be commodities. However, marketing has transformed them into consumer goods.

5   Word study

1. e   2. i   3. k   4. l   5. a   6. j   7. c   8. m   9. h   10. n   11. g   12. d
13. f   14. b

Part 2: Selling tactics

Listening tapescript

A: Look, I'm afraid I'm very short of time.
B: Of course. I understand. I'll only take a few minutes. Could I start by asking you one or two questions?
A: Please do.
B: Well, could you tell me what sort of correspondence goes out from this company?

A: Oh the usual things – quotes, replies to enquiries, publicity material, training material . . .

B: And how much per day?

A: It's difficult to say. Probably about twenty to thirty items each evening.

B: But that could be more when you're doing a mailshot for example?

A: Oh yes, then it's as many as two hundred. But that's only two or three times year.

B: I see. And would you mind telling me who deals with the post?

A: Well, usually my secretary.

B: So she goes down to the post office at the end of each day to weigh up the mail and get the stamps etc?

A: Yes, that's right, it's a nuisance. It takes her a good twenty minutes and the post office is just opposite.

B: I can appreciate that. I'm sure she'd welcome some way of cutting down on that time?

A: Well, yes perhaps she would. But we're only a small firm.

B: That's true. Though it's often the secretary who's most needed in a small firm, wouldn't you say?

A: Absolutely right. She holds the place together.

B: I'm sure she'd appreciate the chance to cut down on such a menial task. As you can see from the literature, we offer just the machine for you – the AK50 – it'll weigh and frank your mail and then anybody can pop it in the post on their way home. Another benefit is that you can print a company logo or sales message on every envelope at no extra cost . . .

2 Listening

In Chart 7.4:

a. Quotes, replies to enquiries, publicity and training material

b. 20–30 items per day (over 200 two or three times per year)

c. Secretary

d. iii ✓

e. Reducing time to deal with post

f. They are only a small firm (limited resources)

g. AK50 franking machine

h. Prints company logo or sales message on every envelope

3 Comprehension/interpretation

3.1 Soft-sell, customer-oriented, listening, leading.

3.2 Perhaps he should have picked up more on the objection that the firm is only small.

4 Language focus

4.1 Question techniques

1. Why don't you have a computer?
2. Could you tell me how many employees you have?
3. You plan to take on more employees (don't you)?
4. You're finding business difficult recently (aren't you)?
5. Do you have any problems recruiting staff?
6. Could you tell me if you pay over the market rate?

7. Could you tell me whether/if you have fired anybody recently?
8. You're a director (aren't you)?
9. Are you facing severe financial difficulties?
10. Could you tell me whether/if you intend to stay in business any longer?

5 Word study

1.	b, f, l, o, r	5.	g, j
2.	c, m	6.	e, k, p
3.	a, h, i	7.	q, s, t, u
4.	d, n		

6 Transfer

B: You are the office manager of a firm of lawyers. You have agreed to meet a salesperson from a coffee machine company. You are short of time. Use the information below to answer the salesperson's questions. Decide whether to purchase.

Situation:

No. of employees: 8 partners (lawyers), 4 assistants, 2 secretaries, 1 receptionist

No. of visitors: Max. 20 a day

Present coffee-making facilities: instant coffee made from boiling water or go out to coffee shop just opposite the office

Problem:
Poor quality coffee for visitors
Time wasted in going out for coffee

Need:
Reliable, good quality coffee-making facilities.

Objections:
Cost: maximum budget £40

UNIT 8
International marketing

Section A: *Entering foreign markets*

Part 1: Ways of entering a foreign market

2 *Reading*

In Chart 8.1

	Advantages	*Disadvantages*
1.1	Little investment, little risk	Less presence and control
1.2	Heavier investment	More presence and control
2.1	Little risk	Less control, danger of creating a competitor
2.2	Quicker start, less risk, form partnership	Less control over process, profitability
2.3	Politically or economically necessary	Disagreement over crucial issues
3.	Lower labour, raw material and distribution costs, better image locally, better local relationships, full control of investment and marketing	Political and economic climate can change

3 *Comprehension/interpretation*

3.1 Because the world economic and political situation is perhaps more changeable and joint ventures represent a more flexible option. Also because there is a move towards conglomeration in many major industries.

3.2 Up to you!

4 *Language focus*

4.1 **Make** and **do**

1. We made the mistake of setting up a joint venture.
2. There's a lot of work to do before setting up in a foreign country.
3. He did the job of importing goods from the Far East.
4. The government made us register the company locally.
5. If we had done our homework, we wouldn't have made the investment.
6. It's important to make friends in high places.
7. Deals like that are made on the ground. You can't do business with these people without meeting them.

8. We could do without interference from politicians but we are making the best of the situation.
9. He did very well to establish the business. It's a pity he didn't make more money.
10. In order to make this work, we're going to have to do a lot of research.

4.2 Verb + preposition

1. They put a lot of money into the project.
2. The project had to be put off due to production delays.
3. Once we had got into the joint venture, it was very difficult to get out of it.
4. Companies are often unwilling to give up their independence.
5. I'd like to take up your offer of collaboration.
6. The company was put off by the size of the investment. They decided instead to go for/ into partnership with a local firm.
7. They made up for their lack of financial investment by doing a lot of the ground work.
8. We could only pull out of the joint venture if they gave up their position in the market.

5 Word study

France	Frenchman/woman	French
China	Chinese	Chinese
Japan	Japanese	Japanese
Brazil	Brazilian	Portuguese
Spain	Spaniard	Spanish
Sweden	Swede	Swedish
UK	Briton	English
Germany	German	German
Netherlands	Dutchman/woman	Dutch

Part 2: Learning from mistakes in foreign markets

Listening tapescript

A: We've put a lot of money into breaking into the European market and now, two years on, we've got very little to show for it. I'm determined to learn from our mistakes. I suggest we look in detail at the three markets we have concentrated on. Edward, why don't you start with France?

B: Basically I feel our results would have been better if we'd relied less on agents and done a bit more active selling ourselves. In the first place it seems we didn't choose our agents well. As you know, we've had to replace two of them. I know it would have been more effort to send our people over, but at least they know the product well. The agents really haven't got a feel for what we're selling.

A: So what you're saying is that we should have taken more active involvement in the sales side?

B: Yes, that's right. We basically under-estimated the sort of product knowledge you need to really sell our line of products.

A: Okay. Janet, you've been looking after Germany.

C: With Germany, I think we've misunderstood the nature of the market. If I'd known how conservative German customers were going to be, I would have recommended a joint venture with a well established German company right from the start. They like to deal with someone on the ground who they know. It would take us years to establish a presence in this market just by going to the trade fairs, and advertising as we've done. I still think it's not too late. I've built up some good contacts and one firm in particular would be interested in some form of joint venture.

A: Right, Janet. We seem again not to have done sufficient research before we tried to enter the market. Roger, what about Sweden.

D: Well, it's a very sophisticated market. We've been trying to enter it by focusing our attention on small to medium-sized companies. In hindsight, this was a mistake. If we'd managed to get an account with one of the large multinationals, I think we'd be well on our way. Although it's sophisticated, everybody knows everybody and word of mouth counts for a lot. We should have concentrated on one or two key prospects rather than going for a lot of smaller fish. Again, I think we've learnt our lesson and I'm optimistic about our future prospects.

A: Thanks, Roger. Well, let's see what we can achieve with a much reduced budget over the last five months of this year . . .

2 Listening

Chart 8.2

Country	Strategy	Mistake	Recommendation
France	Used agents	Didn't choose them well	Use own salesforce with good product knowledge
Germany	Trade fairs	Didn't cooperate with local company	Agree a joint venture with German company
Sweden	Targeted small to medium-sized companies	Should have targeted 1 or 2 large multinationals	Adopt this policy

3 Comprehension/interpretation

Suggestion:

1. a   2. c   3. b   4. d   5. e   Discuss your answers.

4 Language focus

4.1 Conditional III

1. If we had done research beforehand, we wouldn't have made so many mistakes.
2. We would never have entered the market if we had known the problems.
3. In hindsight, we would have done better if we had concentrated on big firms.
4. Looking back on it, we would have penetrated the market if we hadn't used agents.
5. If only I had known, I would never have recommended it.
6. We would not be where we are today, if we hadn't taken risks.

4.2 Chairing

1. c   2. f   3. i   4. a   5. e   6. b   7. j   8. g   9. d   10. h

5   *Word study*

1. d   2. b   3. g   4. i   5. c   6. h   7. f   8. a   9. j   10. e

Section B: Global versus local marketing

Part 1: The world's champion marketers: the Japanese?

2   *Reading*

1. F   2. F   3. F   4. T   5. F   6. F   7. T   8. F

3   *Comprehension/interpretation*

Up to you!

4   *Language focus*

4.1   Determiners: **a/an, the,** ∅

The economy is moving into *a*/∅ recession. This is characterised by ∅ high inflation, ∅ rising unemployment and *a* very low growth rate. What is particularly worrying is *the* large number of bankruptcies that have been reported. It seems that ∅ firms are going into ∅ liquidation at *an* alarming rate. *The* major reason for this is *the*/∅ high interest rates. During *the* eighties, firms grew rapidly, and in order to finance ∅ growth they borrowed *a* lot of money from *the*/∅ banks. Now in *a* time of contraction, they are unable to repay *the* loans.

4.2   Determiners: **much/many, little/few**

1. There are *fewer* natural resources in Japan than most developed countries.
2. *Few* Japanese firms are looking for quick profits.
3. There isn't *much* information about internal strategy.
4. There's too *little* information about Japanese long-term plans.
5. *Much* higher investment is needed by European companies if they want to compete against the Japanese.
6. There is *less* long-term planning in the US than in Japan.
7. There are many *fewer* US companies established in Japan than vice versa.
8. In my opinion, there is too *much* talk and too *little* action.

5   *Word study*

1. e   2. h   3. i   4. l   5. a   6. n   7. m   8. b   9. j   10. c   11. f   12. k
13. g   14. d

Part 2: Corporate versus subsidiary strategy

Listening tapescript

A: So, that briefly outlines our strategy. To summarise, we aim to achieve two major objectives during the next two years; firstly a strong corporate identity throughout the world, and secondly diversification into our three main business areas – health care, industrial chemicals and agricultural products – in all our subsidiaries and affiliates throughout the world.

B: That is very interesting and I can see the benefit to the group as a whole. What worries us here in Japan is that, firstly, a strong corporate identity based around an American company name and logo is not going to help sales here, and secondly, our success in the health care sector is strongly linked to a Japanese profile and not an international profile and I can't see how we can use this profile to diversify into other business areas such as industrial chemicals.

A: I appreciate your concern but I think you have to see that our Japanese business cannot stand alone. The Japanese market is different, of course – all markets are different but the world is getting smaller, and I'm sure you'd agree a truly global presence is what is needed. It'll help to establish our name and reputation for quality in all our business areas.

B: Yes, Mr Stone, we can see that. But we'd like you to consider some of the special factors which affect our business here in Japan – firstly our sales in pharmaceuticals are excellent and they are associated with a long-established Japanese name – our marketing strategy has always been developed to meet the needs of Japanese doctors and Japanese patients. I'm sorry to put this so bluntly but they will not respond well to an American name and image. To put it another way, we know that many Japanese doctors are not aware that we are now owned by an American company and it's best if it stays that way.

A: Sorry to interrupt Mr Tokaido. We see the Japanese market as a key target for our industrial chemicals and agrochemical products. We need the bridge of our name in health care to break into these markets.

B: I really don't think it will help. These are very well segmented markets. There won't be any carry-over from health care to industrial chemicals in any case.

A: There, if you don't mind me saying, you're wrong. Our experience throughout the world is that a strong company image counts for a lot, and associations in one sector carry over into another . . .

2 Listening

Chart 8.3

Corporate strategy:
Objective 1: A strong corporate identity throughout the world
Objective 2: Diversification into three main business areas

Local objections to:
Objective 1: An American identity will not help sales in Japan
Objective 2: No connection between different business areas

---

3   Comprehension/interpretation

3.1   Probably not, he has already decided what he wants to say; he doesn't really listen.
3.2   Probably not, he seems too defensive.
3.3   Try to adopt a more cooperative stand leading to a shared commitment.

4   Language focus

4.1   Participation in meetings

1. c, k   4. e
2. g   5. b, h
3. f   6. a, d, i, j

5   Word study

1. low profile
2. to be integrated/to stand together
3. recently established/newly established
4. absence
5. (very) poor results
6. to be unaware
7. a mass, non-segmented (market)
8. weakly/tenuously linked/connected
9. to consolidate
10. to contract
11. to suffer from

GLOSSARY

A

access (n) available entry; *access to the market*
account executive (n) an advertising executive who looks after a particular client
acquire (v) to buy; *to acquire a company*
    acquisition (n) act of buying; *acquisition of a company*
across-the-board (adj) running an ad for five days
advertise (v) to announce that something is for sale
    ad (n informal) short for advertisement
    advertisement (n) notice or announcement that something is for sale
    advertiser (n) person or company which advertises
    advertising (n) business of announcing that something is for sale; *she's in advertising*
age group (n) category by which target consumers are classified according to age; *the product appeals to the 25–35 age group*
agent (n) person who represents a company
AIDA Attention, Interest, Desire, Action
air time (n) time given to advertising on TV or radio
appeal (n) being attractive
area (n) a region; *his sales area is the North East*
art director (n) person responsible for creative work in an advertising agency
artwork (n) drawings, photographs, etc. used for an advertisement, brochure, publicity material, etc.
assortment (n) combination or range of goods; *the wholesaler's assortment is too wide*
audience (n) people who watch or listen to a TV or radio programme; *this ad will not reach its target audience*
awareness (n) being conscious of something; *the advertisement increased customer awareness*

B

banner (n) material on which an advertising message is printed; *there were banners stretched between the houses advertising the festival*
bargain (n) 1. agreement on price; *he strikes a hard bargain*   2. something cheaper than usual; *that car is a real bargain*
battle (n) fight; *there's a circulation battle between the two newspapers*
behaviour (n) people's habits and customs; *we must analyse consumer behaviour*
below-the-line (adj) below-the-line advertising; advertising which is not paid for
benefit (n) the advantage that a product brings to the consumer; *the main product benefit was a reduction in time*
bias (n) prejudice, lack of objectivity; *focus interviews are subject to interviewer bias*
bleed 1. (n) print that runs to the edge of the page   2. (v) to run print to the edge of the page
body copy (n) main part of an advertising text
Boston Matrix (n) type of product portfolio analysis invented by the Boston Consulting Group
bottleneck (n) a restriction in normal flow; *we've got a bottleneck in our supply operations*
bottom 1. (n) lowest point; rock-bottom price   2. (v) to bottom out; to reach the lowest point
brand (n) a product which can be recognised by a name
    brand leader (n) brand with the biggest market share
    brand loyalty (n) customer desire to continue buying the same brand
    branding (n) the process of giving brand names to products

break even (v) to balance sales and costs, not to make a profit or a loss; *we only just broke even*
        breakeven point (n) point at which sales balance costs
bridge (v) to print an ad across the centre of a double-page spread
brief 1. (n) objectives for a campaign given by an advertiser to an agency   2. (v) to explain to
      people before an assignment; *the salesforce were briefed about the campaign*
broadsheet (n) large sized newspaper (as opposed to tabloid)
brochure (n) publicity booklet; *they asked for a brochure about our services*
budget 1. (n) plan of forecast income and expenditure; *we drew up a pessimistic budget for the
      next six months*   2. (v) to plan forecast income and expenditure
burst (n) a large number of ads over a short period; *we could advertise in a burst or take it more
      slowly*
by-product (n) product which results from manufacturing a main product

call 1. (n) visit; *the salesman plans to make seven calls*   2. (v) to call on someone; to visit
    3. (v) to call someone; to telephone
cannibalism (n) a process when one product reduces the sales of another produced by the same
      company
canvass (v) to visit people to seek their opinions; *we canvassed our customers about the proposed
      new product*
caption (n) short description attached to a photograph or illustration
captive (adj) not free; *the patients in the waiting room are a captive audience for advertisements*
capture (v) to take; *we captured 20 per cent of the market*
cartel (n) group of companies that get together to fix price or control the market
catalogue (US: catalog) (n) a sales publication which list products and prices
cater for (v) to be equipped to deal with; *we can only cater for twenty people*
ceiling (n) highest level; *we are going to have to agree a price ceiling*
chain (n) series of shops belonging to one company
challenger (n) company which enters a market where others are already established
channel (n) means by which goods pass from one place to another; *the main distribution channel
      is through supermarkets*
charge (n) payment for a service; *there is no service charge included in the bill – it is at your
      discretion*
chart (n) diagram which visually displays information
      bar chart (n) uses column height to show variation
      flow chart (n) shows process from first to last step
      pie chart (n) shows data in a circle cut up into segments
checkout (n) place where goods are paid for in a shop
c.i.f. cost, insurance and freight
circular (n) a copied leaflet which is sent to many people
      circulation (n) number of copies of a newspaper sold
classify (v) to put into categories
      classified ads (n) advertisements which are grouped together under certain headings,
          e.g. property, personal
client (n) person or company that buys a service
close (v) to bring to an end; *to close a sale*
cold (adj) not approached before; *a cold call*

colour supplement (n) glossy magazine which accompanies a newspaper

commercialise (v) to make something make money; *they have a good research reputation but they find it difficult to commercialise their products*

commission (n) money paid to the seller, a percentage of the sales made; *we offered the agent a 10 per cent commission*

commodity (n) goods sold in very large quantities, such as metals, foodstuffs

compete (v) to try to do better than another person/company; *it's difficult to compete with low-priced imports*

> **competition** (n) process of trying to do better; *the competition is very fierce*
>
> **competitor** (n) person-company which competes
>
> **competitive** (adj) of a product which competes well; *it's important to keep a competitive edge*
>
> **competitiveness** (v) process of being competitive

complementary (adj) completing, adding to or extending; *toothbrushes and toothpaste are complementary products*

complimentary (adj) given as a gift; *we received two complimentary tickets for Wimbledon*

concentrated marketing (n) marketing directed at one segment of the market

concept (n) business idea; *What is the concept which lies behind the product?*

consign (v) to send goods to a particular buyer

> **consignment** (n) a group of goods sent in one load

consortium (n) a group of companies which work together

> **consumer durables** (n) expensive items which last a number of years, e.g. washing machines
>
> **consumer goods** (n) goods bought by consumers as opposed to industry
>
> **consumerism** (n) process of protecting the rights of consumers

contract (n) legal agreement between two or more parties

> **contract manufacturing** (n) agreement which allows an overseas manufacturer to make your goods

copy (n) text of an advertisement

copywriter (n) person who writes copy for advertisements

corporate (adj) referring to the whole company; *corporate advertising sells the company not its products*

counter (n) flat surface in a shop used for displaying goods and serving customers

> **over-the-counter drugs** retail sales as opposed to prescription sales
>
> **under-the-counter** illegal

coupon (n) piece of paper used instead of money; *as part of the promotion we are offering pre-paid coupons*

coverage (n) proportion of a market which is reached; *we achieved very good coverage with the evening TV ads*

creaming (n) fixing a high price to get high, short-term profits

credit (n) time given between receiving goods and paying for them; *we should give them only three months' credit*

> **creditworthy** (adj) able to buy goods on credit

customer (n) person-company that buys goods

> **customise** (v) to adapt a product for a particular customer

cut-price (adj) sold at a lower price than usual

cut-throat (adj) fierce, intense; *cut-throat competition*

cycle (n) a regularly repeated sequence; *this is our normal selling cycle – it's always quiet after Christmas*

D

dead (adj) no longer active; *a dead account*

deadline (n) date by which something has to be done; *There's no time! Today's the deadline!*

deal (n) business agreeement or arrangement; *we set up a deal with an agent in Houston*

    dealer (n) person-company who buys and sells; *the manufacturer has dealers through-out the country*

    dealership (n) right to buy and sell certain products

    deal with (v) 1. to organise; *I'll deal with that order*   2. to do business with; *we don't deal with middlemen*

delete (v) to remove from the range; *the range is too wide, we'll have to delete some products*

deliver (v) to transport goods to a customer

demand (n) need for goods; *there's not much demand for these products*

department store (n) large store divided into sections selling different types of products

depot (n) a warehouse

depth (n) different forms in a product line

design (n) drawing of a product/advertisement before it goes to production

differentiation (n) making sure that a product has distinguishing features

direct export (n) selling direct to an overseas customer

direct mail (n) selling a product by sending information through the post

direct selling (n) selling direct to a customer without going through any middlemen

directory (n) reference book containing listings; *a telephone directory, a trade directory*

discount 1. (n) percentage reduction from the full price   2. (v) to reduce prices

    quantity discount (n) discount for large quantities

    trade discount (n) discount to wholesaler or other middleman

discretionary (adj) which can be done if you want; *discretionary income is what is left after you have made all your essential payments*

dispenser (n) machine which automatically provides food, drink and other items

display 1. (n) showing or exhibiting goods; *there was a display of the latest research at the trade fair in Frankfurt*   2. (v) to show or exhibit

    display advertisement (n) ad which stands out from other ads because of typeface, border, etc.

distribute (v) to send out goods from the manufacturer to the end-user

diversify (v) to extend into new business areas; *although we are a chemicals company, we diversified into publishing*

    diversification (n) act of diversifying

divestment (n) the selling of product lines or companies

dog (n) term used in Boston Matrix to describe a product with low market growth and low market share

domestic (adj) referring to the home market

door-to-door (adj) going from house to house; *a door-to-door salesman*

dormant (adj) not active at the moment, sleeping; *I'm sure we can awaken some dormant accounts*

down-market (adj/adv) cheap, low end of the market; *to go down-market*

duopoly (n) only two competitors in a market

E

editing (n) correcting, modifying a text or a film
> **edition** (n) an issue of a publication; *this month's edition has an article about roses*
> **editorial** (adj) referring to the editor; *sometimes editorial publicity is much more effective than advertising*

elastic (adj) can change easily; *demand is very elastic – it will not hold up if we increase the price*

end-user (n) person who actually uses a product or service

endorse (v) to say that a product is good; *a professor endorsed our new drug*
> **endorsement advertising** advertising which uses famous people to endorse products

entrepreneur (n) person who starts and runs a company/business

environment (n) area which surrounds a company (both physically and commercially)

escalate (v) to increase rapidly; *prices have escalated recently*

excess (n) amount which is more than permitted
> **excess capacity** more production capacity than is needed for current demand

exhibit 1. (n) thing which is shown at a trade fair or show   2. (v) to display products at a show
> **exhibition** (n) show of goods

expand (v) to get bigger; *the market is expanding*
> **expansion** (n) increase in size

expertise (n) specialist knowledge

exposure (n) 1. publicity given to a product or company   2. total number of audience reached by an advertisement

F

face-lift (n) improvement in the look of a product or a company, suggests the change is only on the surface; *the company has had a corporate face-lift but nothing radical has changed*

facing (adj) opposite; *we'd like the ad put on the facing page*

factor (n) an aspect which must be considered; *price is an important factor when deciding our strategy*

fad (n) a fashion, usually short-lived

family (n) group of products linked by name or packaging

feasibility study (n) investigation of a project to see if it is worth pursuing

feature (n) 1. an article in a publication that deals with a certain subject   2. an aspect of a product, e.g. an alarm system on a car

field (n) outside the office; *the salesmen are in the field*

firm (n) a business or partnership

fix (v) to agree or set something; *the price was fixed at $25*

flagship (n) the main or most successful product in a range

flier (n) a promotional leaflet

flood 1. (n) large quantity; *a flood of orders*   2. (v) to fill with a large quantity; *the market was flooded with cheap imitations*

flop (n) failure; *the product was a flop*

focus group (n) a small group of potential consumers who form part of a market survey

follower (n) company which follows others into a market

forecast 1. (n) an estimate of what will happen in the future   2. (v) to estimate what will happen

format (n) layout of a page

four Ps Product, Price, Place, Promotion

fragment (v) to break into small parts; *the market has fragmented since the competition reduced prices*

franchise 1. (n) licence to sell under a brand name   2. (v) to give a licence to someone

> **franchisee** (n) person who pays a royalty for a franchise

> **franchiser** (n) person who receives the royalty

freebie (n informal) a give-away, a free promotional product

freesheet (n) a newspaper for which there is no cover charge – it is financed only by advertising

freeze (n) a period when nothing changes; *a price freeze*

> **freeze out** (v) to prevent other companies from entering or staying in a market

frequency (n) how often something happens; *we plan to spend more on the ads but use them with lower frequency*

galley (n) first proofs before a text is made into pages

gap (n) a hole, an unfilled space; *there's a gap in the market*

generic (adj) belonging to a type or class; *it's cheaper to buy generic products rather than branded ones*

gimmick (n) an attractive and clever idea; *the agency thought of a publicity gimmick*

giveaway (n) a free PR gift

glut (n) over-supply of a product; *there is a glut of oil*

going rate (n) the market price for a product

goods (n) products, items for sale

goodwill (n) reputation of a business, an intangible asset

gross (adj) total, with no reductions

> **gross profit** (n) sales minus direct costs

grow (v) get bigger

> **growth** (n) increase in size

gutter (n) where two pages meet in the middle of a book or magazine

handle (v) to deal with something; *we can easily handle more business*

hard sell (n) aggressive selling

hire purchase (n) method of buying something by paying over an extended period

hit (v) to reach a target; *we hit the target audience*

hype (n) exaggerated statements in advertising; *I never believe all the hype*

imitate (v) to copy; *me-too products imitate their competitors*

impact (n) strong effect; *the ad had tremendous impact*

impulse (n) sudden decision; *if we want to reach the impulse buyers we need good point-of-sale promotion*

incentive (n) something which motivates; *we need to offer incentives to people joining the company*

indent (v) to start a line of type several spaces in from the left-hand margin

---

index (n) a statistical analysis of a collection of figures, especially average prices

industrial (adj) referring to manufacturing work; *industrial marketing is very different from consumer marketing*

inelastic (adj) not easily changed; *demand is very inelastic so we can increase prices considerably*

informant (n) person who answers questions in a market survey

inhouse (adj) within a company; *all our advertising is done inhouse*

insert (n) something which is put inside something else; *the brochure included a price insert*

introduce (v) to bring a product onto the market; to launch a new product

        introductory offer a special low price to introduce a new product

issue (n) edition or number of a publication; *Have you seen the latest issue of Newsweek?*

itinerary (n) places to be visited on a journey; *his itinerary took him all over the world*

jingle (n) a catchy tune used in advertising

journal (n) a professional publication

junk mail (n) direct mail advertising which is unrequested and usually unwanted

key (adj) important, main; *this client is a key account*

knock (v) to criticise; *knocking other people's products is never a good way to sell your own*

knockdown (adj) very low; *these knockdown prices are unbeatable*

know-how (n) knowledge about how something works

label (n) a small piece of card or material attached to product to show name, price, etc.

laggards (n) category of customers in product life cycle who are very slow to buy

latent (adj) dormant, hidden, waiting to appear; *latent demand*

lateral (adj) to the side; *lateral diversification*

launch 1. (v) to introduce a new product on the market   2. (n) introduction of new product; *the launch was very successful*

layout (n) arrangement of text and illustrations on the page

lead (v) to be the first or the best; *the company leads the world in design*

        leader (n) market leader

leaflet (n) small sheet of printed paper used to advertise

letterhead (n) name and address of a company printed on correspondence paper

licence (US: license) (n) official permission to do something

        under licence (adv) manufactured only with permission

        licensee (n) person who has permission to sell, manufacture, etc.

        licensor (n) person who gives the licence

life cycle (n) concept of showing the different stages in a product's life; *growth is the first stage in the cycle*

lineage (n) way of measuring cost of classified ads by number of lines

literature (n) written information; *please find enclosed our literature about the product*

livery (n) a company's own design used on vehicles, buildings, uniforms

logo (n) design or group of letters used by a company as a distinguishing mark

loyalty (n) sense of belonging and trusting; *customer loyalty*

magazine (n) regular news or special interest publication printed on glossy paper with many photographs

mailshot (n) sending of one campaign of direct mailing

make (n) brand or type of product

manage (v) to control and be in charge of; *to manage a sales office*

> **management** (n) controlling and running a business or part of business; *management by objectives*

> **managerial** (adj) referring to managers; *at a managerial level*

manufacture (v) to make a product using machines

> **manufacturer** (n) company which makes products

> **manufacturing** (n) process of producing; *manufacturing industry*

margin (n) difference between sale price and cost price

> **gross margin** (n) difference between total cost (including overheads) and sale price

market (n) 1. place where a product can be sold   2. possible sales of a product

> **down-market** (adj/adv) cheap end of the market

> **market leader** (n) dominant company or product in the market

> **market niche** (n) small part of specialised market

> **market penetration** (n) amount a product sells in a market

> **market segmentation** (n) division of the market into consumer groups

> **market share** (n) percentage of a total market which one company or product holds

> **market survey** (n) an investigation into a market

> **mass-marketing** (n) marketing aimed at a large undifferentiated customer group

> **up-market** (adj/adv) luxury end of the market

mark up (v) to add an amount to the cost price to reach the sale price

> **mark-up** (n) amount added to the cost price to reach the sale price; *the retailer's mark-up*

mature (adj) fully developed; *mature stage in a product life cycle*

media (n) means of communicating a message

> **mass media** (n) means of communicating to general public, e.g. TV, radio newspapers

> **media buyer** (n) person who places advertisements on TV, radio and in newspapers

> **media coverage** (n) reports about an event in the media; *we need good media coverage for the launch of this product*

> **media planning** (n) decisions about which type and how much

merchandising (n) managing the display and promotion of goods in shops

middleman (n) person/company who acts as an intermediate step between manufacturer and customer; a wholesaler is a middleman

milk (v) to make as much profit as possible; *we should milk the product at this stage in its life*

mission (n) long-term objectives and philosophy of a company; *mission statement*

mix (n) combination of different things; *the marketing mix consists of many elements such as price, promotion, product, etc.*

monopoly (n) a market situation where one company is the only supplier of a product or service

MRP manufacturer's recommended price

N

net (adj) after all deductions have been made; *net profit*
network (n) system which links different parts together; *a distribution network*
niche (n) small segment of specialised market

O

observation method (n) market research method based on watching consumers
obsolescent (adj) going out of date because of advances in technology or changes in taste
obsolete (adj) no longer used; *the product is now obsolete*
offer (n) statement that you are willing to pay something; *we are always open to offers*
    offer (v) to say you are willing to pay/help
off-season (adj) in the cheap, less busy season
operate (v) to run or work a machine/business
    operating profits (n.pl.) profits which result from day-to-day business
opportunity (n) chance to do something; *there are opportunities and threats in this market*
organise (v) to plan and operate something so that it works efficiently
    organisation chart (n) diagram of position of people in a company
orientation (n) direction or main area of interest; *market-oriented company*
outdoor advertising (n) advertising in the open air
outlet (n) a place where something can be sold; *a retail outlet*
overheads (US: overhead) (n) non-attributable day-to-day costs of running a business
own-label (adj) term used to describe goods specially produced for a retailer

P

package (n) a quantity of goods wrapped and sent by mail
    packaging (n) material used to wrap goods for display or for mailing
page (n) one side of a sheet of printed page
    full-page advertisement (n) advertisement taking up a full page
    half-page advertisement (n) advertisement taking up half a page
pamphlet (n) small booklet of advertising information
parcel (n) quantity (usually small) of goods wrapped and sent by mail
patent (n) official registration of a new invention
    patented (adj) protected by a patent
peak (n) highest point
peg (v) to fix prices at a certain level
penetrate (v) to get into a market
    penetration (n) percentage of a target market that is reached
periodical (n) serious (often scientific or academic) publication which appears regularly
pilot (n) a test which will be extended if successful; *a pilot project*
pipeline (n) channel of flow; *Are there any new products in the pipeline?*
pirate (n) person who illegally copies an invention or copyright product; *a pirate copy of the compact disc*
pitch (n) salesperson's talk to persuade a prospective buyer
point of sale, POS (n) place where a product is sold

policy (n) way of doing something; *What is the company policy on discounts?*

poll (n) survey of sample group; *an opinion poll*

portfolio (n) collection; a product portfolio – range of company products

position (n) place or way a product is perceived in a market

    positioning (n) creating an image for a product in a particular sector of a market

poster (n) large notice/advertisement pasted on building or billboard

PR Public Relations

premium (n) 1. amount added to price for a prestige product   2. amount paid for insurance

press (n) newspapers and magazines

    local press (n) regional newspapers

    national press (n) nationally distributed newspapers

    press relations (n) PR activity aimed at building good contacts with journalists, etc.

price (n) money paid for a product

    market price (n) price which people are willing to pay

    pricing policy (n) price paid by final customer

    retail price (n) price paid by final customer

primary data (n) data which must be obtained by active research; raw data upon which no analysis has been performed

prime (adj) most important; *advertisements are most expensive at prime times*

print run (n) number of copies printed; *the longer the print run the cheaper the unit price*

product (n) thing which is made/manufactured

    product portfolio (n) collection of products offered by the same company

    productivity (n) measurement of output per worker

profile (n) characteristics; *customer or market profile*

profit (n) money made from the sale of a product or service

    profit margin (n) percentage difference between costs of sales and income

    profitability (n) amount of profit made as a percentage of costs

    profit centre (n) part of a company which is considered separately when calculating profit

projected (adj) planned/forecast

promote (v) to advertise

    promotion (n) all means of communicating a message about a product or service

    promotional (adj) used in a sales or advertising campaign; *a promotional price has been set 10 per cent lower*

propaganda (n) use of the media to convey a biased political message

prospectus (n) sales document which tries to convince the customer, usually taking a serious approach, e.g. for private schools

prototype (n) first model of a new product

public (adj) referring to people in general

    public sector nationalised industries

    publics (n) groups of people categorised for PR purposes; *the company has many different publics including the local community, the press and their customers*

publication (n) thing which has been published – a book, magazine, etc.

publicity (n) the process of attracting the attention of the general public to products or services

    publicise (v) to attract people's attention by informing them; *the audience was small because the concert had not been publicised*

pull strategy (n) a process of persuading end-users to buy so that middlemen must stock your goods

purchase 1. (n) something which has been bought; to make a purchase   2. (v) to buy
  purchaser (n) person who buys for a company
  purchasing department (n) part of the company responsible for buying raw materials
   and other goods
push strategy (n) a process of persuading middlemen to stock your goods and to help in the selling
 of the product to the end-user

quality (n) the value/worth of a product/service
  quality control (n) checking that the quality is high enough
  qualitative (adj) referring to quality; qualitative research is based on opinions rather
   than facts
quantitative (adj) referring to quantity; quantitative research is based on measurable data
quarterly (n) a magazine which is published four times a year
question marks (n) products in the top-right quandrant of the Boston Matrix which have a low
 market share in a rapidly growing market
quota (n) a limit on the amount of goods which can be imported/exported
quote (v) to estimate the costs; *we were asked to quote for the contract*
  quotation (n) estimate of how much something will cost

R&D Research and Development
random (adj) done without any system; *we used a random sample for testing*
range (n) a series of products from which the customer can choose
rapport (n) good understanding between people; *there is a good rapport between the marketing
 and sales managers*
rate (n) money charged for a certain time or at a certain percentage
  fixed rate (n) charge which cannot be changed
  going rate (n) the usual rate of payment
rating (n) value given to something compared with its competitors; *I'd give them a high rating*
  ratings (n) lists of TV or radio programmes according to the size of audience
  rationalisation (n) process of streamlining a company's operations to gain greater
   efficiency and scale economies
  rationalise (v) to make more efficient, to streamline
raw (adj) in its original, unprocessed state
  raw materials (n) substances used as a base for manufacturing
reach 1. (n) the number of people who see an advertisement once   2. (v) to get to an audience
readership (n) the quantity of people who read a publication
readvertise (v) to advertise again; *we had to readvertise the job*
real (adj) true
  in real terms actually; *prices have gone up 5 per cent in real terms*
recall (n) ability to remember an advertisement
receipt (n) a piece of paper showing that money has been paid or something received; *a receipt for
 items purchased*
recognise (v) to know somebody or something by sight or voice
  recognition (n) brand recognition – ability of a consumer to recognise a brand

recommended retail price, RRP (n) price at which the manufacturer recommends a product is sold to the end-customer

refund 1. (n) money paid back   2. (v) to pay back money; *the money will be refunded if the goods are faulty*

register (v) to record officially

      registration (n) process of recording on an official list; *product registration*

rep (n) short for a representative

repeat (v) to do something again

      repeat orders (n) orders from a customer for more of the same goods over a period of time

repositioning (n) changing the consumers' perception of a product or a service

represent (v) to act on behalf of a company

      representative (n) a salesperson

resale (n) selling goods which have been bought once already

research (n) finding facts and information; market research

resistance (n) a negative feeling towards a product or service; *we encountered a lot of resistance in the market*

respond (v) to reply

      respondent (n) a person who answers questions in a survey

      response (n) answer to a question

retail 1. (n) sale of goods to the end customer   2. (v) to sell goods direct to customers

      retailer (n) person who sells goods direct

return (n) the profit gained from an investment; *we can expect a good return on this project*; return on investment

revenue (n) income received

risk (n) chance of failure

      risky (adj) dangerous

rival (n) a competitor

rocket (v) to rise rapidly

ROI return on investment

rough (n) a sketch of an advertisement

royalty (n) money paid to an inventor/creator/writer by the licensee or publisher

sale (n) act of selling

      salesperson (n) person whose job is to sell the company's goods or services

sample 1. (n) a specimen of a product used to show what it is like   2. (v) to try out something; *we sampled the whiskey before buying it*   3. (v) to test a product on a small group of a target audience

saturate (v) to fill something completely; *the market is saturated*

      saturation (n) a stage in a market's development where there is no room for further growth

scale (n) system of grading; *the scale of the horizontal axis is from 1 to 20*

      scale up/down (v) to increase/decrease size

scarce (adj) not common, rare

screening (n) evaluating, shortlisting

seasonal (adj) only happens in certain seasons; *ice cream sales are very seasonal*

secondary data (n) research data which have already been collected and are available on data banks, etc.

sector (n) part of the economy or industry; *the high-tech sector is growing fast*

segment 1. (n) a section of the market   2. (v) to divide a market into different parts

    segmentation (n) division of the market into segments

sell-by date (n) date on a food packet indicating last date that the food is guaranteed to be good

service 1. (n) the work of dealing with customers; *the service is excellent, we never have to wait*

    2. (n) maintaining a machine in good working order; *the photocopier is due for a service*

    services (n) benefits which do not involve production, e.g. training, transportation

settle (v) to agree; *we settled on a price of $400*

share (n): **market share** percentage of a market held by a company or a product

shelf-life (n) length of time a product can be displayed for sale

skimming (n) setting a high price in order to maximise profits in the short term

slash (v) to cut sharply

slogan (n) a phrase which is used to sell a product; '*A Mars a day helps you work, rest and play*'

slot (n) time for a TV or radio commercial; *we booked five 30-second slots*

slump (n) rapid decrease; *a slump in sales*

societal (adj) referring to society; *societal marketing*

soft-sell (n) selling by argument and encouragement rather than strong pressure to buy

sole (adj) only; *sole distributor*

sourcing (n) obtaining goods from suppliers; *dual sourcing is more secure than single sourcing*

space (n) advertising space; space in a publication for advertising

speciality (n) particular interest; *you will only find certain items in a speciality store*

spending power (n) having money to spend on goods

spin-off (n) a product or service which is developed as a result of a main product; a secondary product

sponsor (n) person or company which pays for an event (sports, culture, etc.) in return for advertising

    sponsorship (n) act of sponsoring

spot (n) a time on TV which is used for advertising

spread (n) two facing pages of a publication used for an advertisement

stagnation (n) not making progress, remaining constant

stand (n) an area for display at an exhibition

sticker (n) piece of gummed paper to be stuck onto articles as an advertisement

storyboard (n) drawings which illustrate a TV advertisement in its planning stage

strategy (n) future action to achieve objectives

    strategic (adj) referring to a plan of action

subcontract (v) to arrange with another company to do some work

    subcontractor (n) company which does work for main contractor

subliminal advertising (n) advertising which conveys a message using subconscious impressions

subscribe (v) to pay in advance for a number of issues of a publication or for membership to a society or club

    subscriber (n) person who subscribes

subsidiary (n) a company which is at least 51 per cent owned by a parent company

subsidise (v) to support financially; *the government has subsidised nationalised industry*

    subsidy (n) money given to support a company/organisation

supplement (n) special additional part of a magazine or newspaper

supply 1. (n) providing products or services; *supply and demand*   2. (v) to provide a service or product
>   **supplier** (n) person or company which provides products or services

surcharge (n) extra charge

surplus (n) having more stock than needed

survey (n) an investigation of a particular market

SWOT analysis (n) analysing a company or project by its strengths, weaknesses, opportunities and threats

synergy (n) producing better results by working together rather than separately

tactic (n) step taken as part of carrying out a strategy

tailor (v) to design something for a special purpose; *tailor-made products*

target 1. (n) figure or point to aim at; *our sales targets are high*   2. (v) to aim at; *we have targeted the 30–45 age group*

tariff (n) tax or charge paid to enter a market; *the EC tariff barriers*

teaser (n) advertisement which attracts by giving very little information – it makes the audience curious

telesales (n) selling over the telephone

tender 1. (n) offer for a certain price; *we have submitted a tender for the project*   2. (v) to offer a price

territory (n) sales or business area

testimonial (n) statement praising a product or service; *testimonial advertising uses statements from satisfied customers*

track record (n) experience and results of a company or person over a number of years; *his track record speaks for itself*

trade in (v) to give back an old product in part payment for a new product; *I traded in my BMW for a Mercedes*

trade mark (n) registered name or design which cannot be used by another company

trend (n) general development or direction; *there is a downward trend in sales*

undifferentiated (adj) having no unique feature
>   **undifferentiated marketing** (n) appealing to all sectors of the market

unique (adj) having no imitations; unique selling proposition (USP)

unstructured interview (n) an interview with no planned structure/questions

up-to-date (adj) current, modern

update (v) to bring up to date

up-market (adj/adv) expensive, targeted at luxury end of the market

upturn (n) a movement upwards; *there has been a marked upturn in sales*

value (n) how much something is worth

variable (n) factor which will change results; *there are too many variables to take into account*

variation (n) amount by which something changes; *seasonal variations account for much of the drop in sales*

variety (n) a range of things; *the wholesaler stocks a variety of products*

vending (n) selling

> **vendor** (n) person or company who sells

venue (n) place where an event takes place; *we have chosen an out-of-town venue for the conference*

vertical (adj) straight up and down; *vertical marketing systems involve integrated systems from manufacturer to retailer*

viewer (n) person who watches television

voice-over (n) spoken comments during a TV commercial given by a person not appearing in the advertisement

voucher (n) paper coupon given instead of money

warehouse (n) building where goods are stored

weekly (n) publication which appears once a week

weighting (n) process of giving more importance to one factor when analysing figures

white goods (n) products such as refrigerators and washing machines used in the kitchen

wholesale (n/adv) buying goods from a manufacturer and selling on to retailers

> **wholesaler** (n) person/company that buys from manufacturers and sells to retailers

wrapper (n) material which wraps a product